Field Guides to Finding a New Career

Education

The Field Guides to Finding a New Career series

Education

By Amanda Kirk

Checkmark Books®
An imprint of Infobase Publishing

Field Guides to Finding a New Career: Education

Checkmark Books
An imprint of Infobase Publishing
132 West 31st Street
New York NY 10001

Library of Congress Cataloging-in-Publication Data

Kirk, Amanda.
    Education / by Amanda Kirk.
        p. cm.—(Field guides to finding a new career)
        Includes bibliographical references and index.
    ISBN-13: 978-0-8160-7597-3 (hardcover : alk. paper)
    ISBN-10: 0-8160-7597-2 (hardcover : alk. paper)
    ISBN-13: 978-0-8160-7621-5 (pbk : alk. paper)
    ISBN-10: 0-8160-7621-9 (pbk : alk. paper)
1. Teaching—Vocational guidance—United States—Juvenile literature.
2. Education—Vocational guidance—United States—Juvenile literature. I. Title.
    LB1775.K548 2009
    371.10023'73—dc22

                                                    2008031369

Checkmark Books are available at special discounts when purchased in bulk quantities for businesses, associations, institutions, or sales promotions. Please call our Special Sales Department in New York at (212) 967-8800 or (800) 322-8755.

You can find Facts On File on the World Wide Web at http://www.factsonfile.com

Produced by Print Matters, Inc.
Text design by A Good Thing, Inc.
Illustrations by Molly Crabapple
Cover design by Takeshi Takahashi

Printed in the United States of America

Bang PMI 10 9 8 7 6 5 4 3 2 1

This book is printed on acid-free paper.

Contents

Introduction: Finding a New Career

Today, changing jobs is an accepted and normal part of life. In fact, according to the Bureau of Labor Statistics, Americans born between 1957 and 1964 held an average of 9.6 jobs from the ages of 18 to 36. The reasons for this are varied: To begin with, people live longer and healthier lives than they did in the past and accordingly have more years of active work life. However, the economy of the twenty-first century is in a state of constant and rapid change, and the workforce of the past does not always meet the needs of the future. Furthermore, fewer and fewer industries provide bonuses such as pensions and retirement health plans, which provide an incentive for staying with the same firm. Other workers experience epiphanies, spiritual growth, or various sorts of personal challenges that lead them to question the paths they have chosen.

Job instability is another prominent factor in the modern workplace. In the last five years, the United States has lost 2.6 *million jobs*; in 2005 alone, 370,000 workers were affected by mass layoffs. Moreover, because of new technology, changing labor markets, ageism, and a host of other factors, many educated, experienced professionals and skilled blue-collar workers have difficulty finding jobs in their former career tracks. Finally—and not just for women—the realities of juggling work and family life, coupled with economic necessity, often force radical revisions of career plans.

No matter how normal or accepted changing careers might be, however, the time of transition can also be a time of anxiety. Faced with the necessity of changing direction in the middle of their journey through life, many find themselves lost. Many career-changers find themselves asking questions such as: Where do I want to go from here? How do I get there? How do I prepare myself for the journey? Thankfully, the Field Guides to Finding a New Career are here to show the way. Using the language and visual style of a travel guide, we show you that reorienting yourself and reapplying your skills and knowledge to a new career is not an uphill slog, but an exciting journey of exploration. No matter whether you are in your twenties or close to retirement age, you can bravely set out to explore new paths and discover new vistas.

Though this series forms an organic whole, each volume is also designed to be a comprehensive, stand-alone, all-in-one guide to getting motivated, getting back on your feet, and getting back to work. We thoroughly discuss common issues such as going back to school, managing your household finances, putting your old skills to work in new situations, and selling yourself to potential employers. Each volume focuses on a broad career field, roughly grouped by Bureau of Labor Statistics' career clusters. Each chapter will focus on a particular career, suggesting new career paths suitable for an individual with that experience and training as well as practical issues involved in seeking and applying for a position.

Many times, the first question career-changers ask is, "Is this new path right for me?" Our self-assessment quiz, coupled with the career compasses at the beginning of each chapter, will help you to match your personal attributes to set you on the right track. Do you possess a storehouse of skilled knowledge? Are you the sort of person who puts others before yourself? Are you methodical and organized? Do you communicate effectively and clearly? Are you good at math? And how do you react to stress? All of these qualities contribute to career success—but they are not equally important in all jobs.

Many career-changers find working for themselves to be more hassle-free and rewarding than working for someone else. However, going at it alone, whether as a self-employed individual or a small-business owner, provides its own special set of challenges. Appendix A, "Going Solo: Starting Your Own Business," is designed to provide answers to many common questions and solutions to everyday problems, from income taxes to accounting to providing health insurance for yourself and your family.

For those who choose to work for someone else, how do you find a job, particularly when you have been out of the labor market for a while? Appendix B, "Outfitting Yourself for Career Success," is designed to answer these questions. It provides not only advice on résumé and self-presentation, but also the latest developments in looking for jobs, such as online resources, headhunters, and placement agencies. Additionally, it recommends how to explain an absence from the workforce to a potential employer.

Changing careers can be stressful, but it can also be a time of exciting personal growth and discovery. We hope that the Field Guides to Finding a New Career not only help you get your bearings in today's employment jungle, but set you on the path to personal fulfillment, happiness, and prosperity.

How to Use This Book

Career Compasses

Each chapter begins with a series of "career compasses" to help you get your bearings and determine if this job is right for you, based on your answers to the self-assessment quiz at the beginning of the book. Does it require a mathematical mindset? Communication skills? Organizational skills? If you're not a "people person," a job requiring you to interact with the public might not be right for you. On the other hand, your organizational skills might be just what are needed in the back office.

Destination

A brief overview, giving you an introduction to the career, briefly explaining what it is, its advantages, why it is so satisfying, its growth potential, and its income potential.

You Are Here

A self-assessment asking you to locate yourself on your journey. Are you working in a related field? Are you working in a field where some skills will transfer? Or are you doing something completely different? In each case, we suggest ways to reapply your skills, gain new ones, and launch yourself on your new career path.

Navigating the Terrain

To help you on your way, we have provided a handy map showing the stages in your journey to a new career. "Navigating the Terrain" will show you the road you need to follow to get where you are going. Since the answers are not the same for everyone and every career, we are sure to show how there are multiple ways to get to the same destination.

Organizing Your Expedition

Fleshing out "Navigating the Terrain," we give explicit directions on how to enter this new career: Decide on a destination, scout the terrain, and decide on a path that is right for you. Of course, the answers are not the same for everyone.

Landmarks

People have different needs at different ages. "Landmarks" presents advice specific to the concerns of each age demographic: early career (twenties), mid-career (thirties to forties), senior employees (fifties) and second-career starters (sixties). We address not only issues such as overcoming age discrimination, but also possible concerns of spouses and families (for instance, paying college tuition with reduced income) and keeping up with new technologies.

Essential Gear

Indispensable tips for career-changers on things such as gearing your résumé to a job in a new field, finding contacts and networking, obtaining further education and training, and how to gain experience in the new field.

Notes from the Field

Sometimes it is useful to consult with those who have gone before for insights and advice. "Notes from the Field" presents interviews with career-changers, presenting motivations and methods that you can identify with.

Further Resources

Finally, we give a list of "expedition outfitters" to provide you with further information and trade resources.

Make the Most of Your Journey

Your decision to embark on a new career is probably not a choice that you made lightly. It takes courage, drive, and resourcefulness to leave behind the familiar and set your course toward new employment horizons. Those are all qualities that will serve you well in the field of education. Whether you decide to teach, counsel, or take on an administrative role, you will be playing a vital part in determining the nation's collective future. The education that the next generation receives today affects greatly the kind of world we will live in tomorrow. All levels of education, from preschool to continuing education for adults long out of the traditional classroom, have a vital role to play in shaping our character, our skills, and our intellectual curiosity.

In this volume, you will find an overview of some of the types of jobs that are available in education today. New technological innovations, as well as new ideas in pedagogy, are continually increasing the variety of jobs available. If you are interested in moving into the vast field of education, there is likely a position out there that will build on your current skill set and employment experience.

The traditional classroom teacher is probably the first job that comes to mind when you think of education-related careers. With everyone from toddlers to seniors taking classes today in a seemingly endless variety of subjects, from geology to video game design, there are many teaching options that you could pursue. Let us consider them chronologically: If you enjoy babysitting and take pleasure in the wide-eyed wonder and enthusiasm of small children, you might find preschool or kindergarten teaching appealing. A roomful of three- to six-year-olds can be exhausting, but the rewards of helping them develop important social skills and physical coordination, as well as laying a good foundation for their academic pursuits can be enormous. The next level of education for children, and another area of teaching that you might be attracted to, is elementary school, which comprises grades one through five (six in some districts). As an elementary school teacher, you give your students a basic foundation in reading, writing, and arithmetic, as well as art, history, and social studies. The transition from playing full-time to sitting at a desk and paying attention to the teacher is often a difficult one for young children, so the work of helping students acquire social skills continues throughout elementary school and forms a significant part of a teacher's work. The next phase of education, and the next level of teaching that you might consider, is middle school, which varies by district from grades six through eight or grades seven through nine. Teachers at this level begin to specialize in one subject, such as math, science, English, or social studies, and the expected skill level is higher since students are beginning to learn intermediate concepts in these fields. Middle schools are more likely than elementary schools to offer language classes, and to have dedicated teachers in the arts, including drama and music, and physical education. Course offerings will vary by school, and are closely linked to financial resources. Middle school students are entering the universally awkward phase of adolescence, which poses unique challenges for teachers, but shepherding students through the important academic and social choices they make at this juncture in their lives can be gratifying.

Next comes high school, a level of education that presents new challenges and rewards for both students and teachers. As a high school teacher, you will specialize in one subject, which you may teach at a variety of levels from freshman through senior honors/Advanced Placement. Your skills in the subject you teach will need to be at a fairly high level, and an advanced degree in your field will be an asset in getting a job. High school teachers have the important role of launching their pupils out into the world as adults, and the mentoring they provide can shape the course of a student's life and future career. High school teachers are often asked to write letters of recommendation for college applications. College, the next level of education, is another employment option for prospective teachers to consider. At this level of teaching, subject areas are highly specialized, and an advanced degree, such as a Ph.D., is usually required. Some fields, such as business, law, public policy, and journalism, are particularly open to career-changers who bring real life experience to the classroom.

For many of us, education does not end with a university degree. People continue to take classes in areas of interest, or to keep work-related skills up to date, for the rest of their lives. Informal and part-time teaching options are increasingly available at adult learning centers, community centers, and other venues that offer classes and certifications. If you would like to apply your current job skills to a teaching position, this is something to consider. Other teachers that work outside the traditional classroom environment include tutors and special education teachers. The tutoring business has grown in recent years as anxious parents are eager to give their children every advantage in preparing for college. Tutors can also offer remedial assistance to pupils who are falling behind their grade level in a given subject. Special education teachers provide one-on-one individualized curricula to pupils with mental or physical disabilities. Some special education teachers work with students who attend mainstream classes; others work with students whose disabilities necessitate a special classroom environment tailored to their mental or physical limitations. The road to becoming a special education teacher is a long one, as getting a job requires obtaining a degree, passing exams to receive certification, and completing several years worth of internships.

An area of teaching that requires slightly less preparation is teaching English as a foreign or second language, sometimes referred to as TEFL or ESL teaching. A variety of certification programs are widely available, and the courses are relatively short and inexpensive. If you long to set sail for distant ports, dropping anchor in different destinations, English teaching could be the job for you. With English language skills a prerequisite for many jobs, most non-English-speaking countries have language schools that are eager to hire native speakers. English teachers are also in demand in American schools that serve large numbers of children of immigrants, such as in the Southwest.

Teaching is not the only career option in the field of education—far from it. Librarians, for example, serve a critical function in the modern education system. The availability of reference materials for students and researchers is continuously increasing, as is the variety of new media that houses this information. Someone has to keep up with the changing technology, and ensure that the information is accessible. This is the job of the modern-day librarian, whose work has less to do with shelving books than managing databases. Librarians in schools sometimes have the opportunity and obligation to teach, offering classes in ouline research skills and new technologies, and they must attend continuing education classes to keep up with the latest technological developments. Being a librarian today is a dynamic and critical job, so do not let outdated stereotypes of cardigans and glasses on chains dissuade you from this exciting career.

Another non-teaching career in the world of education is that of guidance or school counselor. This is a perfect job for someone with a background in psychology or counseling, who would like to employ their skills to work with children in a context that will have a measurable impact on them. There are several types of counselors employed by schools at different grade levels. Guidance counselors usually work with high school juniors and seniors. They direct students towards higher education and job opportunities that fit each student's talents and interests. Depending on the school, a guidance counselor may be working in conjunction with parents to get their charges into top schools, or focusing on preventing attrition and guiding pupils toward community colleges and technical and trade schools. Guidance counselors can also work with younger students to help them choose courses, internships, and extracurricular activities that will steer the pupil toward his or her chosen career destination. Other types of school counselors help to treat students with addictions and behavioral problems, and recognizing students who may be facing a neglectful or abusive home environment. They work with medical professionals and special educators to get students appropriate assistance and intervention.

Last, but certainly not least, school administrators work behind the scenes like the production crew of a play to ensure that the school is adequately funded and maintained, and that legal requirements are being met. There are many types of administrators at grade school level, from district superintendents who oversee the running of many schools, to principals and vice principals at each individual school, human resources staff who oversee hiring, compensation, and benefits for faculty and staff, engineers who maintain the physical aspects of the school and its grounds, and assorted other administrative roles. Colleges and universities have their own extensive systems of administration, including the higher echelons of school executives, such as presidents, chancellors, provosts, and deans, to student affairs and admissions personnel. If you take the time to explore available opportunities in school administration, at both the grade school and university levels, you may find that your current skills will help you segue into an interesting new career.

Self-Assessment Quiz

1: Relevant Knowledge

1. How many years of specialized training have you had?
    (a) None, it is not required
    (b) Several weeks to several months of training
    (c) A year-long course or other preparation
    (d) Years of preparation in graduate or professional school, or equivalent job experience

2. Would you consider training to obtain certification or other required credentials?
    (a) No
    (b) Yes, but only if it is legally mandated
    (c) Yes, but only if it is the industry standard
    (d) Yes, if it is helpful (even if not mandatory)

3. In terms of achieving success, how would rate the following qualities in order from least to most important?
    (a) ability, effort, preparation
    (b) ability, preparation, effort
    (c) preparation, ability, effort
    (d) preparation, effort, ability

4. How would you feel about keeping track of current developments in your field?
    (a) I prefer a field where very little changes
    (b) If there were a trade publication, I would like to keep current with that
    (c) I would be willing to regularly recertify my credentials or learn new systems
    (d) I would be willing to aggressively keep myself up-to-date in a field that changes constantly

5. For whatever reason, you have to train a bright young successor to do your job. How quickly will he or she pick it up?
   (a) Very quickly
   (b) He or she can pick up the necessary skills on the job
   (c) With the necessary training he or she should succeed with hard work and concentration
   (d) There is going to be a long breaking-in period—there is no substitute for experience

II: Caring

1. How would you react to the following statement: "Other people are the most important thing in the world?"
   (a) No! Me first!
   (b) I do not really like other people, but I do make time for them
   (c) Yes, but you have to look out for yourself first
   (d) Yes, to such a degree that I often neglect my own well-being

2. Who of the following is the best role model?
   (a) Ayn Rand
   (b) Napoléon Bonaparte
   (c) Bill Gates
   (d) Florence Nightingale

3. How do you feel about pets?
   (a) I do not like animals at all
   (b) Dogs and cats and such are OK, but not for me
   (c) I have a pet, or I wish I did
   (d) I have several pets, and caring for them occupies significant amounts of my time

4. Which of the following sets of professions seems most appealing to you?
   (a) business leader, lawyer, entrepreneur
   (b) politician, police officer, athletic coach
   (c) teacher, religious leader, counselor
   (d) nurse, firefighter, paramedic

5. How well would you have to know someone to give them $100 in a harsh but not life-threatening circumstance? It would have to be...
   (a) ...a close family member or friend (brother or sister, best friend)
   (b) ...a more distant friend or relation (second cousin, coworkers)
   (c) ...an acquaintance (a coworker, someone from a community organization or church)
   (d) ...a complete stranger

III: Organizational Skills

1. Do you create sub-folders to further categorize the items in your "Pictures" and "Documents" folders on your computer?
   (a) No
   (b) Yes, but I do not use them consistently
   (c) Yes, and I use them consistently
   (d) Yes, and I also do so with my e-mail and music library

2. How do you keep track of your personal finances?
   (a) I do not, and I am never quite sure how much money is in my checking account
   (b) I do not really, but I always check my online banking to make sure I have money
   (c) I am generally very good about budgeting and keeping track of my expenses, but sometimes I make mistakes
   (d) I do things such as meticulously balance my checkbook, fill out Excel spreadsheets of my monthly expenses, and file my receipts

3. Do you systematically order commonly used items in your kitchen?
   (a) My kitchen is a mess
   (b) I can generally find things when I need them
   (c) A place for everything, and everything in its place
   (d) Yes, I rigorously order my kitchen and do things like alphabetize spices and herbal teas

4. How do you do your laundry?
   (a) I cram it in any old way
   (b) I separate whites and colors

    (c)   I separate whites and colors, plus whether it gets dried

    (d)   Not only do I separate whites and colors and drying or non-drying, I organize things by type of clothes or some other system

5.   Can you work in clutter?

    (a)   Yes, in fact I feel energized by the mess

    (b)   A little clutter never hurt anyone

    (c)   No, it drives me insane

    (d)   Not only does my workspace need to be neat, so does that of everyone around me

IV: Communication Skills

1.   Do people ask you to speak up, not mumble, or repeat yourself?

    (a)   All the time

    (b)   Often

    (c)   Sometimes

    (d)   Never

2.   How do you feel about speaking in public?

    (a)   It terrifies me

    (b)   I can give a speech or presentation if I have to, but it is awkward

    (c)   No problem!

    (d)   I frequently give lectures and addresses, and I am very good at it

3.   What's the difference between *their, they're,* and *there*?

    (a)   I do not know

    (b)   I know there is a difference, but I make mistakes in usage

    (c)   I know the difference, but I can not articulate it

    (d)   *Their* is the third-person possessive, *they're* is a contraction for *they are,* and *there is* a deictic adverb meaning "in that place"

4.   Do you avoid writing long letters or e-mails because you are ashamed of your spelling, punctuation, and grammatical mistakes?

    (a)   Yes

    (b)   Yes, but I am either trying to improve or just do not care what people think

(c)   The few mistakes I make are easily overlooked

(d)   Save for the occasional typo, I do not ever make mistakes in usage

5.   Which choice best characterizes the most challenging book you are willing to read in your spare time?

(a)   I do not read

(b)   Light fiction reading such as the Harry Potter series, *The Da Vinci Code*, or mass-market paperbacks

(c)   Literary fiction or mass-market nonfiction such as history or biography

(d)   Long treatises on technical, academic, or scientific subjects

V: Mathematical Skills

1.   Do spreadsheets make you nervous?

(a)   Yes, and I do not use them at all

(b)   I can perform some simple tasks, but I feel that I should leave them to people who are better-qualified than myself

(c)   I feel that I am a better-than-average spreadsheet user

(d)   My job requires that I be very proficient with them

2.   What is the highest level math class you have ever taken?

(a)   I flunked high-school algebra

(b)   Trigonometry or pre-calculus

(c)   College calculus or statistics

(d)   Advanced college mathematics

3.   Would you rather make a presentation in words or using numbers and figures?

(a)   Definitely in words

(b)   In words, but I could throw in some simple figures and statistics if I had to

(c)   I could strike a balance between the two

(d)   Using numbers as much as possible; they are much more precise

4.   Cover the answers below with a sheet of paper, and then solve the following word problem: Mary has been legally able to vote for exactly half her life. Her husband John is three years older than she. Next year,

their son Harvey will be exactly one-quarter of John's age. How old was Mary when Harvey was born?

(a)   I couldn't work out the answer
(b)   25
(c)   26
(d)   27

5.   Cover the answers below with a sheet of paper, and then solve the following word problem: There are seven children on a school bus. Each child has seven book bags. Each bag has seven big cats in it. Each cat has seven kittens. How many legs are there on the bus?

(a)   I couldn't work out the answer
(b)   2,415
(c)   16,821
(d)   10,990

VI: Ability to Manage Stress

1.   It is the end of the working day, you have 20 minutes to finish an hour-long job, and you are scheduled to pick up your children. Your supervisor asks you why you are not finished. You:

(a)   Have a panic attack
(b)   Frantically redouble your efforts
(c)   Calmly tell her you need more time, make arrangements to have someone else pick up the kids, and work on the project past closing time
(d)   Calmly tell her that you need more time to do it right and that you have to leave, or ask if you can release this flawed version tonight

2.   When you are stressed, do you tend to:

(a)   Feel helpless, develop tightness in your chest, break out in cold sweats, or have other extreme, debilitating physiological symptoms?
(b)   Get irritable and develop a hair-trigger temper, drink too much, obsess over the problem, or exhibit other "normal" signs of stress?
(c)   Try to relax, keep your cool, and act as if there is no problem
(d)   Take deep, cleansing breaths and actively try to overcome the feelings of stress

3. The last time I was so angry or frazzled that I lost my composure was:
   (a) Last week or more recently
   (b) Last month
   (c) Over a year ago
   (d) So long ago I cannot remember

4. Which of the following describes you?
   (a) Stress is a major disruption in my life, people have spoken to me about my anger management issues, or I am on medication for my anxiety and stress
   (b) I get anxious and stressed out easily
   (c) Sometimes life can be a challenge, but you have to climb that mountain!
   (d) I am generally easygoing

5. What is your ideal vacation?
   (a) I do not take vacations; I feel my work life is too demanding
   (b) I would just like to be alone, with no one bothering me
   (c) I would like to do something not too demanding, like a cruise, with friends and family
   (d) I am an adventurer; I want to do exciting (or even dangerous) things and visit foreign lands

Scoring:

For each category...

For every answer of *a*, add zero points to your score.
For every answer of *b*, add ten points to your score.
For every answer of *c*, add fifteen points to your score.
For every answer of *d*, add twenty points to your score.

The result is your percentage in that category.

Private or Public School Teacher

Private or Public School Teacher

Career Compasses

Get your bearings on what it takes to be a successful private or public school teacher.

Caring about your students and their educational development (30%)

Organizational Skills to plan lessons and keep records for multiple classes (20%)

Communication Skills to teach students at varying ability levels simultaneously (20%)

Ability to Manage Stress, since dealing with children, parents, administrators, and regulations makes teaching a stressful career (30%)

Destination: Private or Public School Teacher

The motivations for pursuing a teaching career are varied but often center on a desire to give back. People who become educators sometimes cite a wonderful teacher of theirs as inspiration; or, having achieved success in their chosen field, they long to share their knowledge and experiences with future generations. Whatever your motivation for making a transition to teaching, it is important to consider both the rewards and challenges of this service-oriented career. Until you receive state certification

2

for teaching in public school, you can still work in private schools and in an array of educational institutions.

Demand for teachers correlates with birthrates and teacher attrition, and both are high in various areas of the United States right now. In particular, there is a growing call for bilingual teachers in areas with many immigrants. Spanish is the most sought-after language, with teachers needed in every subject and at every grade level, including special education (a distinct subfield of teaching with unique certification and degree requirements not covered in this chapter). The high attrition rate for teachers creates continual job openings, but they are not evenly distributed geographically. Retention rates for teachers are lowest in schools that serve economically disadvantaged children, particularly in inner-city districts. Often overcrowded and underfunded, these schools present teachers with multiple challenges.

Since children's needs change so rapidly, career options in the field of teaching are wonderfully diverse. Preschool teachers watch three- or four-year-olds while their parents or guardians are at work. Barely out of toddlerhood, children at this age are not expected to sit at a desk and study academic subjects. Preschool teachers focus on helping their charges develop social skills, creativity, and coordination. Learning is centered around play at the preschool level, but by kindergarten letter and number recognition are expected and the environment begins to become more structured in preparation for elementary school. Teachers at this level in public schools usually have a degree in early childhood education, but private schools often do not require this credential. Kindergarten students usually attend a morning or afternoon session, although some schools offer all-day kindergarten to better accommodate the needs of working families. Teachers usually teach both sessions each day.

Elementary school teachers usually work with first through fifth grades, in which the children are ages five to ten. Structured learning begins in earnest the day children begin first grade, when they must adjust to staying seated at a desk all day. Most elementary school teachers teach a variety of subjects to the same group of students, but practices vary by school. Some schools expect elementary school teachers to specialize by subject or to teach in teams. Specialized subjects outside the general academic curriculum, such as art, music, and physical education, are sometimes taught by a separate teacher, who moves from classroom to classroom.

Middle school teachers face the challenging task of guiding students through the beginning of adolescence, at ages 11 to 13 in grades six through eight. Teachers at this level almost always specialize in one subject, and teach only that subject to several grade levels. Students have already been introduced to basic concepts in math, reading, science, history, and other academic disciplines and are now expected to master intermediate concepts in these subject areas.

Essential Gear

Get certified! All teachers in U.S. public schools must be licensed by a state board of education to teach in the state in which they work. Licensure is usually not transferable between states, but some states have reciprocal agreements, and you can usually get a one-year temporary license to teach in another state. To obtain a teaching license you must have a bachelor's degree, pass a state test (which varies considerably in difficulty from state to state), and complete state-approved and mandated education courses. If you have a degree in education, you most likely have enough general education credits to meet most state requirements; if not you will need to obtain a preliminary license while you take the necessary courses at a local college of education.

Secondary school teachers, who take on the high school years of grades nine through twelve and ages 14 to 18, see their charges blossom from awkward adolescents into young adults. They are the final influence on students before they are thrust out of the cocoon of twelve-plus years of compulsory education into the bewildering array of choices they will face in adult life. Secondary school teachers can exert a strong influence on the educational and career choices that students will make after high school graduation. At this level, teachers specialize in one subject. In addition to the general teaching credentials required by their state and school, most high school teachers have a degree in their subject area, often a master's degree and sometimes even a doctorate.

The teaching environment of American schools varies widely. Some schools, both public and private, offer state-of-the-art audio-visual and computer equipment; extensive art, music, and physical education facilities and programs; support staff such as guidance counselors and teaching assistants; resources for students with special needs; honors and Advanced Placement curricula; funds for field trips and special projects; and other amenities. In other public schools, however, teachers struggle with overcrowded classrooms, inadequate facilities and supplies, outdated textbooks, and a curriculum that focuses excessively on preparation for standardized tests. These less prosperous or progressive private schools may present a challenging teaching environment as well.

The academic calendar is not as uniform as it was in the past. Some schools have gone to a year-round format, with short breaks between each session instead of a summer vacation. Teachers whose schools still follow the traditional academic calendar often teach summer school to make ends meet or are required by their states to attend professional development or continuing education programs during summer vacation.

A teacher's work does not end when the bell rings, nor is it confined to the classroom. Teachers at all levels grade homework, prepare assignments and lesson plans, deal with countless administrative tasks and paperwork, fill out report cards and write progress reports and recommendations for students, and meet with parents. Much of this work is done in the evenings and even on weekends, which means that most teachers work well over a 40-hour week.

Directing classroom focus is Job 1.

Salaries for teachers are usually higher in public schools; they are required to meet standard state criteria to hold their jobs and are represented by a union. Public school teachers' compensation also often includes health insurance, and pension plans are likely to be present and standardized. Education, experience, and seniority all factor into salary, but the earning ceiling for most teachers is low compared to top pay outside of education. Salary goes up by grade level, with preschool teachers earning the least, at around $20,000 per year, and secondary school teachers earning the most, with some public high school teachers in wealthy suburbs earning $70,000.

Demand for new teachers is expected to rise as the baby boomer generation approaches retirement, and the changing demographics of the school-age population will dictate the location and type of job opportunities that will be available. The demand for inner-city and Spanish-speaking teachers at all grade levels and in all subject areas is expected to rise, with most job openings in the South and West and declining job prospects in the Northeast and the Midwest. The shortage of qualified teachers in math and science is expected to keep demand strong in these subject areas, especially at higher grade levels.

You Are Here

You can begin your journey to public or private school teaching from many different locales.

Do you have a degree or employment experience in a commonly taught subject? Teachers in academic subjects often have at least an undergraduate degree in education and, at the secondary school level, a specialization in one subject such as math, English, or history. Teachers of non-academic subjects sometimes have a practical background in a related field rather than a teaching degree; a shop teacher might be a former carpenter, or a home economics teacher might have been a professional cook, seamstress, or tailor. Art and music teachers can fall on either side of this divide, with some having teaching degrees and others being artists or musicians who also teach. Even in academic subject areas, a degree in your field can be an adequate substitute for a teaching background, especially in science and mathematics. A physicist, chemist, biologist, or even a writer or editor with an English degree, would make an excellent candidate to teach these subjects, including in public school, with the right certification.

Do you have a criminal record? Schools are legally obliged to conduct criminal background checks to ensure that they do not hire anyone with a felony conviction or any record related to sex crimes, especially crimes involving children. In the past, schools have only been able to check state records, allowing people with records in other states to obtain teaching jobs that they should not have. Due to technological advances in data sharing, more extensive background checks are increasingly possible. Be sure that you could pass the most stringent background check before even considering a teaching career.

Do you have a lot of patience? Really. Whatever grade level you choose to teach—from preschoolers to high school seniors—your students will try your patience on a daily basis. If the students do not faze you, consider the parents—both those who are maddeningly under- and over-involved in their child's education. Then factor in the school administration and the constraints on your work imposed by local, state, and federal regulations. Pulling your hair out yet? No? Then read on.

Navigating the Terrain

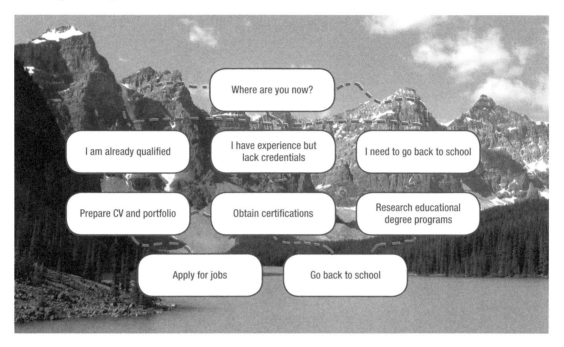

Where are you now?

I am already qualified

I have experience but lack credentials

I need to go back to school

Prepare CV and portfolio

Obtain certifications

Research educational degree programs

Apply for jobs

Go back to school

Organizing Your Expedition

Before you set out, know where you are going.

Decide on a destination. If you are unsure whether you want to teach public or private school, that means private—at least until you acquire the experience, credentials, and requisite certificates to be a teacher in a public department of education. In the meantime—and perhaps to your preference—you will find many private that will appreciate your skills, life experience, and enthusiasm. After giving some thought to setting, ask yourself what age group would you like to teach? Each stage of childhood presents challenges and rewards for teachers. Teaching preschool- and kindergarten-aged children requires tremendous patience and an understanding of the way young children think, but fewer academic skills. Elementary school teachers must help students begin to focus in classes and learn the fundamentals, not to mention sit at a desk all day. Middle school teachers must cope with children beginning adolescence, the most awkward stage of our lives. Secondary school teachers may have students who are bright, motivated, and college-bound, or they may struggle with potential drop-outs who never learned the basics and are floundering in the face of more advanced work. You also need to choose between public and private school employment, weighing differences in teaching environments, curricular freedom, and compensation.

Scout the terrain. Making use of the Internet, look for teaching vacancies in your area. Find out your state's licensing requirements, which you can locate using the Web sites listed at the end of this chapter. Talk to any family members or acquaintances who are teachers and ask them about the rewards and challenges of their jobs. Consider whether you would like to join a program that accepts teachers without prior experience or teaching credentials like Teach for America or New York City Teaching Fellows.

Essential Gear

Be realistic about salary and location. Both demand and salary levels vary widely by subject area, grade level, geographic area, and whether it is a public or private institution. Generally speaking, public school teachers make more money and have more benefits than private school teachers; secondary school teachers are paid more than primary school teachers; and wealthier districts, often in the suburbs, pay their teachers more than poorer districts, usually found in the inner cities and small towns. The availability of jobs reflects this pattern. As a new teacher, you may find more job opportunities in lesser-paid positions in less affluent areas, where job satisfaction among teachers may be lowest and turnover highest.

Find the path that's right for you. The numerous grade levels, subject areas, and types of schools—public or private, religious, technical, or arts-oriented—provide a rich variety of opportunities. It is up to you to find the one that is the right match for your skills and interests. If you were a history major, worked in advertising for 20 years, and now want to teach high school history, go for it! If you feel your lease on life renewed in the presence of small children for whom everything in life is fresh and exciting, then become an early childhood teacher. Depending on which path you choose, you may need to move, go back to school, or make some lifestyle changes to accommodate your dream.

Go back to school. Most people looking to change careers and become teachers will need to go back to school, whether to earn a new degree or to obtain the required education credits for licensure. Depending upon your ultimate career goal, and the teaching needs in your area, you may be able to start teaching on a provisional license while you study part-time, or you may be able to bypass formal certification altogether by teaching in a private school. You might start out in a private school and then, if you discover that you like teaching and would like to widen your job prospects, you may go back to school later. If you decide to embark on a course of study, check first with the National Council for Accreditation of Teacher Education (NCATE) for their list of accredited institutions. (http://www.ncate.org)

Landmarks

If you are in your twenties... You might want to start by getting a degree in education. If you already have an undergraduate degree, you could apply for a program such as Teach for America, or you might consider graduate school. A master's degree will increase your starting salary by several thousand dollars, and open doors to moving into administration, should that direction interest you later.

If you are in your thirties or forties... You should begin by assessing the marketability of your current skill set in the public and private school curriculum. Teaching a subject related to your current field might offset your lack of formal teaching credentials and experience.

If you are in your fifties... Your options vary, depending on your prior educational and employment experience and your financial situation. You might be in a position to parlay your existing skills into a private school teaching job as you take courses to obtain certification, or you may be in a financial position to return to school full-time to pursue a teaching degree.

Notes from the Field

Louisa Gomez
Private high school teacher
San Francisco, California

What were you doing before you decided to change careers?

I was working in a translation office that was allegedly working for the Department of Commerce but, in fact, it was working for the CIA. I was editing translations and translating from Spanish.

Why did you change your career?

My intention was to go into college teaching, but there were no jobs, so I ended up in the translation job. When they closed the San Francisco office, I was out of a job. I wasn't interested in moving to Washington, D.C., so I went to an employment agency and presented my credentials. I went to several, actually, but one of them handled teaching positions and they thought there would be a match for my language skills in a high school teaching job. It wasn't exactly what I was after, but I figured why not try high school teaching.

How did you make the transition?

[I started at] a private high school—private, because I had no teaching credentials. I liked it. This school had really oddball students and that was a lot of fun. I started out teaching French and German and, after

If you are over sixty... Your journey to teaching as a new career will be tied to your destination goals. If you would like to get a full-time job as an elementary or secondary school teacher, you could face some age discrimination, unless you have strong relevant credentials or the ability to teach understaffed subjects like math and science. Potential employers will want to know that you intend to stick around, so emphasize your commitment to your new career and play up any relevant experience or expertise. You might start out as a substitute teacher as you look for appropriate job openings.

Many public school teachers start in private schools.

a while, they decided they wanted me to teach English composition since I was the only one on the staff who knew any English grammar. Then they decided to hire a specialist in French so they gave her the French class. I kept the German and English composition classes. Then they decided to phase out German. Finally, I was teaching ninth grade composition and English literature, and I stuck with that.

What are the keys to success in your new career?

The key to success is being more competent than most of the other people on the staff. I ended up being the interim head of school after they fired the old headmaster. For while I thought I might like to be the permanent head, but I didn't like the administrative work. I decided that I preferred teaching. So I went back to just being academic dean in my spare time from teaching, and I created the computer system for the school, and even served briefly as registrar when the new system was being implemented.

My advice for dealing with students is: Don't scream—speak very softly when you are trying to get them to be quiet, and say something that they want to hear like, "The next one who opens his mouth is dead," but say it very softly. It has gotten so that you really have to entertain them, which is not how it used to be, but for the most part they are pretty interesting.

Further Resources

Teach for America is a program that places both recent graduates and career-changers in schools in low-income neighborhoods. It requires a two-year commitment and willingness to move wherever you are assigned. http://www.teachforamerica.org

USREAP Applications Network provides a one-stop form for applying for teaching and administrative jobs in multiple school districts nationwide. You can select as many districts as you wish, saving the time and hassle of filling out a separate application for each district. http://www.usreap.net

No Child Left Behind This U. S. Department of Education Web site describes the purposes and provisions of this piece of legislation. The site also contains links to other USDE information.
http://www.ed.gov/nclb/landing.jhtml

Teacher Certification Requirements for All 50 States are available on the Web site of the University of Kentucky's College of Education.
http://www.uky.edu/Education/TEP/usacert.html

Librarian- - - - -

Librarian

Career Compasses

Get your bearings on what it takes to be a successful librarian.

Relevant Knowledge of library database systems (30%)

Caring about your patrons and their research needs (20%)

Organizational Skills to facilitate efficient database management (30%)

Communication Skills to deal with patrons whose information needs far exceed their current research skills (20%)

Destination: Librarian

Librarians are the professional drivers of the information superhighway. They chauffeur us with confidence and speed to our information destinations. As the quantity of available information increases, librarians update their ways of classifying it to make it organized and accessible for students, professional researchers in every field from law to health sciences to art, and the public. You tell a librarian what you want to know, and he or she will tell you where and how to find information on that subject. Long gone are the days when libraries contained only resources written on paper, such as books and periodicals. Microfilm, sorry to say, is still around to deepen your crow's feet as you squint at the screen, but today it is merely one roadside attraction on the research trail. Librarians handle everything from DVDs to DNA samples, and from ancient manuscripts to yesterday's presidential speech.

As the field has changed, so has the image of the librarian. Once upon a time, the profession was associated with humorless old ladies in fluffy sweaters with their glasses on chains, and balding men in cardigans, both shushing anyone who dared to so much as squeak a shoe on the polished floors of their domain. Now, the profession has acquired a subtle allure—old school meets technologist.

The job itself has changed along with its image makeover. The work of checking library materials out to patrons, checking them in again, and shelving them is now mostly done by assistants, sometimes known as pages or library technicians. Senior librarians often move up to managerial positions where they oversee library budgets, training of employees, and the upkeep of the facility. There are many jobs in a library that are not done by librarians, but the heart and soul of a credentialed librarian's work is still helping patrons find the information they seek. The biggest changes are in the types of resources available and where they are kept. Most of the information available in a given library is not physically kept on site, let alone out on shelves. Almost all periodicals, for example, are now stored in online databases. This saves space, and trees, but it has transformed a librarian's job from managing books to managing electronic information.

Librarians are a skilled labor force, well trained and well compensated. Librarian jobs in both the public and private sector generally require a master of library sciences (MLS) degree and some require further certification and licensing. Most states require local public librarians to hold state certification, and virtually all public school librarians need to fulfill their state's teacher certification requirements in addition to library-specific credentials. There are a variety of specialized librarians who work in various industries and academic fields. These librarians usually hold degrees in the relevant discipline, such as law or music or medicine, as well as the MLS. Other librarians work on designing the computer databases that hold information; they often hail from the field of computer science and hold degrees in database management, programming, and related areas of information technology. In addition to the initial educational requirements of this career path, librarians must participate in ongoing professional development to keep their skills up to date. Information storage and retrieval systems are constantly changing, and librarians must know them well enough to explain them to patrons as soon as they are available for use.

Essential Gear

A degree in the hand is worth two in the works. While it is true that not all libraries require the MLS degree, having this credential will clear the path to more job options, better salaries, and higher-level appointments. Librarians rely on assistants, sometimes called library technicians, to do the work of data entry and shelving books. An MLS will give you a stronger start in your new career. As part of earning your MLS, you may be required to work as an intern at a library. This is a good opportunity to lay the groundwork for a future full-time job, so be sure to make a favorable impression.

With all of this education, one would anticipate that librarians are well compensated, and usually this it true. School librarians are often paid more than teachers, and some college librarians earn more than the professors at their institutions. The average earnings of a librarian as of May 2006 were $49,060. Public school librarians and those at other public facilities are sometimes unionized, and full-time workers usually have health insurance, pensions, and other benefits. Librarians sometimes work part-time, particularly at libraries that need staff to fill evening and weekend hours, and at small municipal libraries that are only open limited hours. This type of flexibility can make it an appealing career choice for parents who must juggle childcare around both spouses' working hours. School librarians sometimes follow the academic calendar of other teachers, but college and university libraries are often open when school is not in session. School library work is more seasonal than other areas, with some libraries open until midnight or even later during exam times. Librarians who work in a business environment or in a law firm may work the long hours associated with the corporate world.

The working environment of a librarian varies by specialization and library size, but it generally involves a lot of computer time. School and university librarians spend part of their time giving classes and tutorials in how to use their library's reference materials. Whereas such courses once consisted of giving tours of the facility, they now resemble computer-training courses. Larger libraries will have librarians who specialize in a certain collection or type of media, but smaller libraries will expect their sole librarian to be the font of all research wisdom.

Despite the dire warnings in the news about the decline of reading, the employment outlook for librarians in the near term is good. This strong job market is mainly due to a demographic anomaly: More than two-thirds of librarians will be approaching retirement age within the next decade. Career changers should bear in mind that enrollment in MLS programs is also rising, so competition for jobs is expected to increase as well.

The role librarians play in helping people gain access to information is important not just for practical reasons but for ideological ones as well. Librarians choose what books and other media to purchase for their collections, they recommend reading, listening, viewing, and other materials to patrons of various ages, and they strive to make more information accessible in convenient formats every day. A free society only remains such as long as the open exchange of information is facilitated; librarians maintain that ideal.

Librarians have hot computer skills.

Far from being an old-fashioned or sedate career, the field of library sciences is on the cutting edge of technology. Librarians combine the computer skills of a network administrator with the memory of an elephant. With such busy and important jobs, it is a wonder they find any time to read.

You Are Here

You can begin your journey to a career as a librarian from many different locales.

Do you have strong computer skills? In the twenty-first century, much of a librarian's work is done sitting at a computer. In a sense, a librarian is akin to a database manager—a job traditionally categorized under information technology. Many library materials are not physically available in the library but are accessed through online databases. A good librarian knows these repositories of information thoroughly and helps patrons efficiently find the information they seek. While you will become more familiar with the databases that are relevant to your area of specialization over time, you must go into the job with fairly advanced database management skills.

Do you have a related degree or work experience? If you are changing careers to become a librarian, it is unlikely that you already have a master of library sciences; however, there are other degrees and jobs that could be relevant to your new career. Librarians who specialize in a particular field often have a degree in that field. For example, a law librarian will often possess a law degree in addition to the MLS, an art librarian will have a degree in art history, a database designer will have a degree in computer science, and a school librarian often must be a certified teacher with previous classroom teaching experience.

Are you detail-oriented? Remember when your elementary school class went to the library to learn the intricacies of the Dewey decimal system from the school librarian? Later, perhaps in college, you may have learned the Library of Congress classification system. For a librarian, these two common classification schemes are just the tip of the information management iceberg. Every book or other type of reference material that you file has a place in its classification system—an exact place—and the item, and all associated records, must match and be traceable at all times. In the life of a librarian a passion for order will not go unrewarded.

Organizing Your Expedition

Before you set out, know where you are going.

Decide on a destination. Why do you want to be a librarian? Is it for the heart-pounding, adrenaline-pumping action? The dating opportunities? The ability to discreetly delete your overdue fines? Seriously, consider what appeals to you about the profession. It bears similarities

Navigating the Terrain

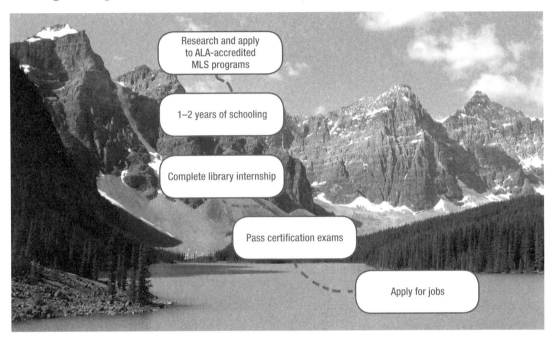

Research and apply to ALA-accredited MLS programs

1–2 years of schooling

Complete library internship

Pass certification exams

Apply for jobs

to teaching, and many librarians teach classes in research skills. Some school and municipal librarians read stories to children. Others work in acquisitions and must keep abreast of all the latest releases in order to effectively augment their library's holdings. Some librarians are archivists who preserve important documents, videos, and other media for future generations. The working environment is usually quiet (and often freezing cold), and the job has its routine aspects, which can be relaxing or tedious, depending upon your perspective. The pace is not always slow. Librarians who assist patrons often face pressure to rapidly locate information. It is a rewarding job, but one whose challenges and quirks should not be lightly dismissed.

Scout the terrain. A large percentage of librarians are approaching retirement age, so most current library vacancies are due to retirement. Using the links provided at the end of this chapter, investigate librarian job openings in your area. Consider both public and private schools, colleges and universities, public libraries, law firms, corporations, media outlets, and government offices. You would be amazed how many types of businesses employ a degreed librarian to manage their reference materials. When you find a position that interests you, determine the job requirements. Do you need an MLS? For most jobs, the answer is yes, but there are exceptions. Are there lower-level jobs within the library hierarchy that you could get while you pursue your MLS? Do any employers provide tuition reimbursement? Do this research before you return to school; it could save you time and money over the long haul.

Find the path that's right for you. There are many types of librarians, and believe it or not, most no longer wear their hair in a bun (although there are still a lot of eyeglasses in the field). Librarians often specialize in one field of reference material, such as art, law, or science. Some have "back office" jobs as database designers or archivists. School librarians can work in environments that range from a one-room elementary school library that is open part-time to a twenty-two-story state university research library. Likewise, a public librarian in a small town will have a different working environment, hours, and duties than a librarian in a major city or one employed by a law firm or corporation. All of these are great jobs for the right person. Think about your financial needs, your geographical flexibility, your interests, and your existing skills, and find the niche that suits you.

Go back to school. A master of library sciences degree is essential for all but the lowest level librarian jobs. Some schools may call it a master of librarianship or a master of library and information studies—that is OK—what matters is that the program is accredited by the American Library Association (ALA). Use the information on each school's Web site to help choose a program that fits your library career goals. Before applying, you will have to take the Graduate Record Exam (GRE), a standardized test, as well as provide undergraduate transcripts and letters of recommendation; you may also have to write an essay and attend a personal interview. Some schools may take it for granted that your computer skills are good and start right in with advanced training that is specific to library work. Be sure that you have strong computer skills before you begin so you do not get in over your head.

Landmarks

If you are in your twenties... You should dive right in and get an MLS degree now. Any undergraduate major offers some preparation for a career as a librarian, but a background in information sciences, database management, or other computer skills will be especially useful. Be sure to ascertain what education courses you need to work in your local school system, as you might be able to obtain those credits while you are in school for your MLS.

Essential Gear

Buckle down to travel the information superhighway. Gone are the days when librarians typed out three cards for each book so that patrons could look them up in the card catalog by title, author, or subject. Not only are library catalogs computerized nowadays, but most library materials are stored in hard drives, not on bookshelves. The greater part of your job will consist of helping library patrons find the information they seek in online databases rather than pointing them to the correct aisle. Your computer skills, especially your research skills, need to be top notch so that you are conducting your charges down the information superhighway in an Audi, not a scooter.

If you are in your thirties or forties... You might want to look into doing the MLS degree part-time over two years. This option would enable you to keep your current job, and give you ample time to prepare for whatever state teaching certification you need as well.

If you are in your fifties... You could be in a position to unmoor yourself from your old career completely and tack into a full-time MLS program. If your previous career involved information management or teaching, you might want to see if any specialized librarian niches might take advantage of your existing skills. Check out the Special Libraries Association for more ideas in this direction: http://www.sla.org.

If you are over sixty... Your path to your new career in library science is the same as that of younger career changers. The difference is that you

Notes from the Field

Sharon Kranzberg
Public high school librarian
Brooklyn, New York

What were you doing before you decided to change careers?

I actually began my career as a teacher, but was soon forced out of teaching by New York City's fiscal crisis in the early 1970s. I started a small home-decorating business, the Shady Lady, which sold and installed window treatments. This was about the time when vertical blinds were becoming popular, and as the "Shady Lady" my business rapidly expanded. I found business to be thoroughly enjoyable.

Why did you change your career?

Perversely, my business became a victim of its own success. It grew to the point that it was too big for me to handle by myself, yet if I hired someone to help me run the business, it would no longer be profitable. I was beginning to run into child-care problems as well. I was looking for some regularity in my life—regular hours, regular paychecks, and regular health insurance.

How did you make the transition?

I knew that I wanted to eventually return to teaching, but I realized that I would have to position myself in a specialty that would not leave me so vulnerable to the fluctuating job market. I looked around at the schools, and spoke to people who had experience with the school systems, and decided that being a school librarian would combine my enjoyment of teaching with having my own niche. If I were to go back to teaching, I would need to complete a master's degree, and becoming a librarian required that I obtain a master's in library science, so these

will be competing with younger workers for jobs in a field that is struggling to integrate new employees during a time of usually high attrition due to retirement. Emphasize the breadth and depth of your acquired knowledge and expertise in diverse fields. Stress your people skills.

two goals meshed very nicely. I attended Pratt Institute in the evenings and got my degree in two years. I had to pass the NYC [New York City] teaching exam in my specialty, and then wait for an appointment to a school. At first, it was a little strange to not have my own regular classes, but I soon realized that being the resource person in the school was an exciting position to be in. My business experience helped me in doing the book ordering, and in adjusting to the fact that being the librarian involved certain administrative tasks, as well as actual teaching. And I do get to teach quite a bit. The library offers classes for all of our students in how to use our online resources. I spend much of my day showing students how to search for articles in our databases, and how to discriminate between reliable and unreliable sources in their online research. The library provides me with a laptop computer to take home, so that I can take online courses to update my own skills.

What are the keys to success in your new career?

The most important thing is to enjoy children, and to understand that each student comes to you with different needs and abilities. In some ways, being a librarian requires as much individualization as choosing the correct window treatment to set off a room. Whereas before, I dealt with colors and styles, now I deal with genres and reading abilities. I also must know how to get along with all the different teachers in my school, and be able to "sell" my program to teachers who might be reluctant to try something new. My job varies between being a teacher who can show a class the best way to accomplish their research and being a cheerleader for books. I have to keep up with what's new in books, what the kids want to read, and sometimes defending my choices of purchases. Overall, I find being a librarian a completely fulfilling experience.

Further Resources

The American Library Association   provides information for aspiring librarians, including lists of accredited degree programs and scholarships. http://www.ala.org/ala/education/educationcareers.htm

Library Job Postings on the Internet is just what it sounds like.
http://www.libraryjobpostings.org/libraryjobs.htm

Resources for School Librarians contains information on degree programs, continuing professional development, school librarian certification, and jobs. http://www.sldirectory.com/libsf/resf/jobs.html

American Association of School Librarians disseminates standards and best practices for school librarians.
http://www.ala.org/ala/aasl/aaslindex.cfm

College Instructor

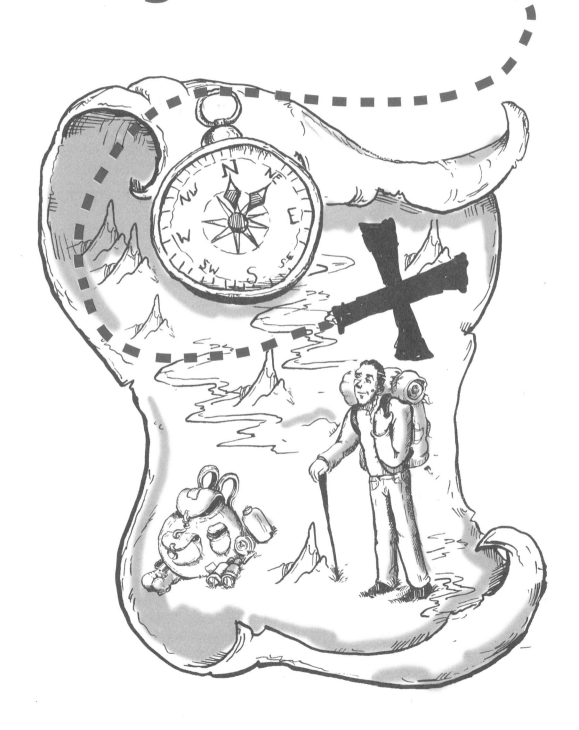

College Instructor

Career Compasses

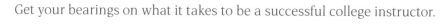

Get your bearings on what it takes to be a successful college instructor.

Relevant Knowledge of the subject you will be teaching (40%)

Caring about your students and their development (20%)

Organizational Skills to keep track of schedules, grade assignments on time, and plan lectures (20%)

Communication Skills to get your ideas across clearly and keep students' interest (20%)

Destination: College Instructor

The title "professor" summons up the image of an intellectual reading, writing, and teaching gifted students in the pristine beauty of an Ivy League campus. If you are considering college teaching, you probably already know that a tenured faculty position at an Ivy League school is not the most common destination in this field. And the journey— even to a part-time teaching position at a junior college—will pose challenges. Still, teaching college students can be a very rewarding experience—especially for those who enjoy communicating ideas and helping others to grow intellectually, professionally, and personally. Other treasures awaiting you at the end of the road include a flexible schedule, summers and school breaks off, and being part of a vibrant and intellectually stimulating environment.

The journey may not be as hard as you might think. While most college professors have Ph.D.s—particularly those in academic subjects such as mathematics, languages, history, English, and science—earning a doctorate is not the only way to reach the college classroom. People with other advanced degrees such as MDs, MFAs, and JDs are also well-equipped to teach. Likewise, those with substantial real-world experience, especially in business, accounting, engineering, or other specialized fields, can blaze their own paths. This especially holds true for those who are considering teaching as part-time work and are not interested in getting on the path to a tenure-track job. *Tenure* is special status granted to a faculty member, usually at four-year schools (although sometimes at two-year colleges), that ensures job security. Tenure is intended to allow college faculty the freedom to say and publish what they believe to be true, rather than having to shape their work to political considerations. After all, for many people, the path to academia is born out of intellectual curiosity and the desire for enlightenment.

So what destinations are open to those who do not intend to end their journey at a tenure-track job? One of the most popular is becoming an *adjunct professor*, that is, a professor who teaches specific classes on contract rather than as a full-time employee of the college. Becoming an adjunct can be a very good strategy for a second-career starter. Those who come to academia late in life often find it difficult to land tenure-track jobs, especially since hiring committees tend to reason that the candidate will have fewer productive years than someone who entered the field at a younger age. However, the terrain of the adjunct can also be an unstable place to pitch your tent: Adjunct instructors are usually contracted to teach from year to year, and even though their contracts may be renewed for many years, adjunct professors have no job security and few benefits.

Nevertheless, academia can be a crowded place. However, the field is expected to grow much faster than average in coming years as many professors retire and the number of college-age students increases. The most growth is expected to be in adjunct and short-term positions; those who can teach subjects that are most in demand—especially professional subjects—will fare best in the job market. This is good news for second-career starters, who may possess specialized knowledge due to their real-life experience.

Adult-education programs and *distance-learning institutions* are also opening up new opportunities for would-be professors. Adult-education is geared toward those older than traditional college age, and is often professionally oriented. Distance learning breaks out of traditional classrooms by delivering instruction remotely, usually over the Internet. Distance-learning classes can meet live by Webcam or by exchanging messages and written work, usually through e-mail.

Essential Gear

Be sure to keep your CV close at hand. The CV (curriculum vitae) is the academic equivalent of the résumé. It should emphasize your academic qualifications and teaching skills, as well as your publications, papers, and service. It is also standard practice to send letters of recommendation and several sample syllabi, or plans for courses you will teach, with each application. Unlike a résumé, a CV can be many pages long.

Make sure you have what it takes to make the journey and to stay there once you arrive. Being a professor is not simply getting up in front of a class and spouting forth wisdom. Organizational skills are critical: You must plan your lectures and present the material in a logical and coherent fashion, while also keeping track of tests, papers, and the school schedule. You may find yourself getting involved in students' lives as they come to you with personal problems or difficulty with course work, or as you develop a mentoring relationship with some of them. There are many other responsibilities that go with the job description. Depending on what sort of teaching you are doing, you may be expected to serve on committees, attend conferences, plan events, perform community service, and publish or exhibit your work.

Be familiar with local customs. For instance, the inhabitants of academia tend to be a technology-savvy lot. Computer skills are essential, as e-mail, online learning technologies, and Microsoft's PowerPoint are often used in the modern classroom. While most applications used in college teaching are similar to what you would use in the business world, some online services, such as WebCT and Blackboard, are specialized educational tools designed to allow professors to post assignments and readings and students to hand in their work electronically. Most are easy to learn and use.

As with so many journeys of self-discovery, the greater part of the rewards in academia are intangible. Do not expect to find King Solomon's mines at the end of the road. Still, while most college professors do not make very much money, the job can be lucrative for those with specialized knowledge and skills. According to the U.S. Department of Labor, the median annual salary was $51,800 in 2004, with the lowest 10 percent making less than $25,460 and the top 10 percent making $100,000 or more. The American Association of University Professors reported an average annual salary of $68,505 in 2004–2005. Those who work in four-year colleges, particularly large, private colleges, tend to earn more than those who work for two-year, smaller, religious, or public schools. Adjunct professors also tend to earn less than regular faculty. Teachers of professional subjects such as psychology, computer science, and business tend to be among the high earners because these courses are much in demand and because schools need to offer high salaries in order to attract potential hires away from the private sector. Shakespeare scholars, historians, and philosophers are rarely lured away from academia by high-paying corporate jobs.

You Are Here

You can begin your journey to academia from many different locales.

Do you have an advanced degree, teaching or work experience, or other qualifications? For many people, the transition to postsecondary education is a logical outgrowth of their current job. For instance, research scientists may find themselves teaching at a large research university, psychologists may become psychology professors, and well-known poets and fine artists may be offered faculty positions at prestigious colleges and universities. Some of these jobs are in two-year vocational programs such as nursing, where a master's degree or the equivalent is sufficient. Other teaching opportunities, in drama or dance, for example, are focused more on achievement and performance than on formal credentials.

Are you working in a specialized field? Many professors, particularly in business programs, have backgrounds in industry and finance. Similarly, lawyers—especially those with less common specialties, such as patent law, family law, and environmental law—can become law professors, and medical doctors can teach in medical schools. For some professionals, such those in the arts (especially those who hold an MFA degree), part- or even full-time teaching can be a way of supplementing their income. Teaching college can also be a good late-career or post-retirement pursuit for those who have distinguished themselves in some field.

Are you interested in exploring a subject unrelated to your past experience? If you would like to teach a subject completely different from the one you are currently working in, or if your field has additional requirements, then you have little choice but to go back to school. Bear in mind, however, that going back to graduate school as an adult is no easy task. See "Organizing Your Expedition" for helpful advice.

Navigating the Terrain

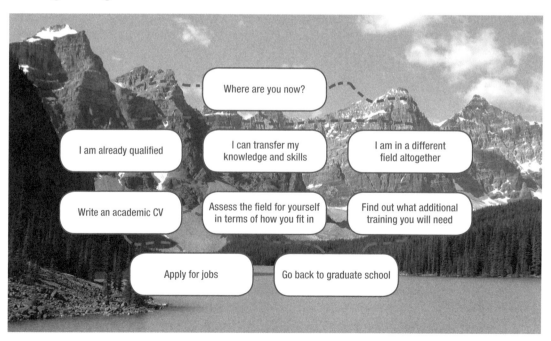

Where are you now?

I am already qualified

I can transfer my knowledge and skills

I am in a different field altogether

Write an academic CV

Assess the field for yourself in terms of how you fit in

Find out what additional training you will need

Apply for jobs

Go back to graduate school

Organizing Your Expedition

Before you set out, know where you are going.

Decide on a destination. Is your goal to be a full-time, tenure-track professor in a four-year university, or a part-time adjunct professor? To teach at a community college, or for a distance-learning institution? Also, is your chosen field something that you are already qualified to teach? Bear in mind that requirements vary quite a bit among different institutions. Some schools are primarily concerned with your teaching abilities, while others put a premium on research and publishing; still others are willing to overlook a lack of advanced degrees or teaching experience in favor of professional work experience. Be realistic, as well: If you have just spent 40 years as a medical assistant, you are not likely to be able to teach art history without substantial additional training. One possibility is to consider teaching at a private high school, which may be more flexible about credentials than public school systems.

Scout the terrain. Look through classified ads on Web sites such as http://www.higheredjobs.com for jobs similar to the sort you would like to have. What qualifications do they expect of applicants? Do you have these qualifications, or can you obtain them? Does a job teaching art or design require a portfolio? Will you have to go back to school for additional education—even moving to another city to attend a program in your field? In this case, you will need to take stock of your personal and financial situation. You should also investigate ways to finance your education, such as grants, loans, and scholarships. Remember that you may need to modify your goals somewhat. Going to school part-time while working is one option. Another is to choose a degree more in line with your original career field—business instead of history, for instance.

To teach what you want, teach what you can.

Find the path that's right for you. There are many paths to the classroom, depending on what you want to teach and where. You may be in for years of struggle in graduate school and a job search, or you may find a job with one phone call to a contact who works at a university. Everybody's case is different; the important thing is to be flexible. Con-

Notes from the Field

Ken Mondschein
College instructor
New York, New York

What were you doing before you decided to change careers?

After college, I spent another year in school to earn my MA in history. After that, I really needed to take a break from academia, so I cast about for something to do. I had always loved books, and I had written for publication and gained some editorial experience in college and grad school, so I decided to go into the New York publishing world. The MA helped me land an editorial position, and I worked in the industry for six years—mostly doing academic textbooks and reference works.

Why did you change your career?

I liked working in publishing—especially the "getting paid on a semi-regular basis" part—but history was always my first love and I'd honestly always intended to go back to graduate school. Still, if it wasn't for one particular incident, I probably would have stayed in publishing. I was working quite happily for a major publisher when we received word that the corporate owners were closing the New York office and centralizing operations to save money, thus causing a number of talented, intelligent, and hard-working people to lose their jobs. This had happened to me several times during my career—publishing is a

sider searching for a job in a field that matches your expertise, rather that spending years training to become an expert in a field that has little to do with your prior experience. Another option is to search for an administrative position in a university that will allow you to take classes for free on a part-time basis.

Go back to school. Surviving graduate school could be a book in itself. Programs range from one- to two-year professional degrees to six-, seven-, and even eight-year Ph.D. tracks followed by years of postdoctoral research. Not only will you have to adjust to studying, writing papers, and taking tests, but you will be cast back into life on a student budget.

notoriously unstable industry. After that, I decided that it was time to go back to grad school.

How did you make the transition?

The first step, in my case, was to apply to graduate history programs. I made a mistake here—I should have researched professors whose interests matched mine and then geared my application to them, rather than simply telling the schools what I was interested in. As it so happened, I did find a professor who shares my interests and a program into which I fit. I also had to re-take the GRE, since your scores expire after a few years. The school helped me apply for student loans, and I also received a fellowship that paid my fees, as well as a small stipend.

What are the keys to success in your new career?

The hardest part is getting a job in the first place, and the trick there is to distinguish yourself as much as possible before you begin the job hunt. What skills and knowledge do you bring to the table? Why are you an expert in this field? I can't emphasize enough that your job hunt begins long before you ever apply for a position. Get as many publications, conference presentations, portfolio pieces, gallery exhibitions, good reviews, teaching experience or whatever else you might need well before you go on the job market. Yes, it sounds very mercenary—but anyone who thinks higher education is all about living in the world of ideas is kidding themselves.

Landmarks

If you are in your twenties... You are in an excellent position to earn admission to graduate school in an academic subject, such as literature or history. In fact, many graduate schools prefer applicants with "real world" experience. There are also some scholarships, such as the Gates Cambridge Scholarship, that are only open to applicants under 30 years of age.

If you are in your thirties or forties... You may face discrimination in your chances for admission, the amount of financial aid offered, and (more informally) in evaluations of your work once you are enrolled. Still you have presumably acquired useful skills and perspectives, as well as self-discipline. Your professional experience may help you survive graduate school as well as bolstering your resume for teaching certain professional subjects such as nursing or business.

Essential Gear

Pack your CV with credentials in order to give yourself the best chance at landing a job. The academic job market can be highly competitive. Publishing books and articles, giving papers at professional conferences, teaching classes (even at extension schools or adult-education programs), having exhibitions of your art or photography, and doing public-service work can all give you the edge on the competition.

If you are in your fifties... You may be well positioned to teach in your field, assuming you have been relatively successful. After all, who better to teach a class on entrepreneurship than a real-estate tycoon, civil rights than an advocacy attorney, interior design than an accomplished designer, or accounting than an accountant with years at a big firm?

If you are over sixty... You may see teaching college as a way to keep your mind sharp and to pass on your skills and experience to the next generation. Though you may be too far down your original path to set out on a new course, you may have all the knowledge and experience needed to teach in your field.

Further Resources

The American Association of University Professors (AAUP) is the largest professional organization of college professors in the nation. http://www.aaup.org/aaup

Grad Student Resources on the Web provides links to some of the best available resources for graduate students. http://www-personal.umich.edu/~danhorn/graduate.html

Preparing Future Faculty is an organization dedicated to preparing the college professors of tomorrow. http://www.preparing-faculty.org

The Association for Career and Technical Education (ACTE) is dedicated to career-oriented education. http://www.acteonline.org

Tutor

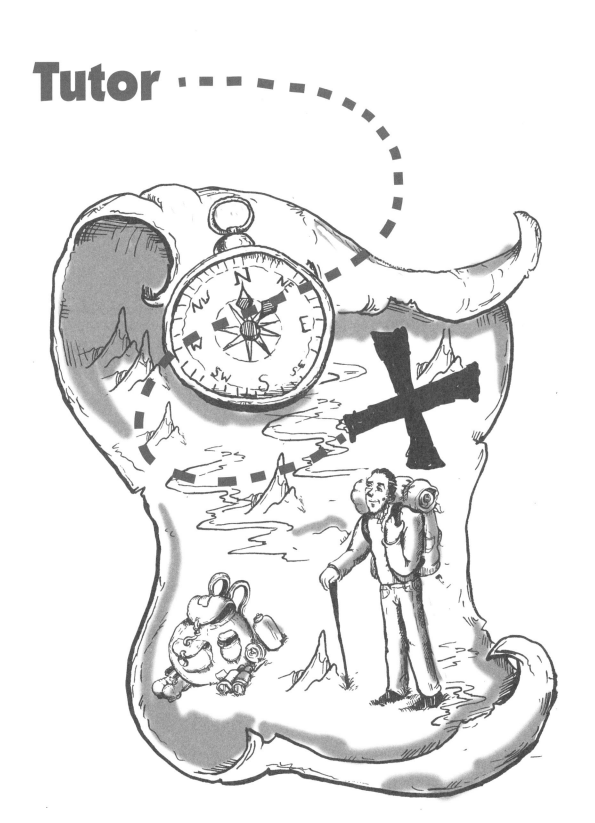

Tutor

Career Compasses

Get your bearings on what it takes to be a successful tutor.

Relevant Knowledge of whatever subject you tutor is the most basic requirement (40%)

Mathematical Skills are useful because math is the subject with the highest demand for tutors (20%)

Organizational Skills are needed to keep track of scheduling and invoicing and to maintain accurate records of goals and accomplishments for each client (20%)

Communication Skills are crucial for reaching students who need one-on-one assistance, and for explaining complex concepts (20%)

Destination: Tutor

If you ever thought that teacher and psychologist seemed like equally appealing careers, you may be well suited to a career as a tutor. A tutor is a teacher who works intensively with students one-on-one, often in an informal setting. Tutors can teach any subject, and they can work with any age group. Some tutors are involved with remedial and special education, helping students who are behind their grade level in certain academic skills. Other tutors are hired by students or their parents so that they can prepare for undergraduate or graduate entrance exams or test out of certain courses. Adults who wish to learn a new skill, such as a foreign language, computer program, or sport, may hire a tutor. The job of tutor is appealing for its flexibility, and most tutors work part-time. It is more viable as a way to supplement your income or fulfill a desire to teach than as a full-time career in itself. Of course, how much time you spend tutoring and how much money you make doing it will depend upon several factors.

Tutors teach in a variety of environments. A tutor can strike out on his or her own, teaching at home, at the client's home, or meeting in a neutral location, such as a café, or outdoors in fine weather. Some tutors rent office space or other facilities that are appropriate for their subject, but this is not usually necessary. Tutors who work for public or private schools often have an office or classroom that they use, and they may be expected to keep hours similar to regular teachers at that school. Another popular option for tutors is to work for a tutoring center, such as a language school or test prep company. These tutors may have office space at their place of employment, or they may be sent out into the field to tutor in clients' homes much as a freelance tutor would do. A relatively new medium is online tutoring. There is considerable debate about the effectiveness of tutoring over the Internet, but the use of online tutoring is growing, especially in academic subjects like writing, math, and science. Online tutors might work "live" with clients in a chatroom setting that mimics face-to-face contact, or they could work off-line to critique work that has been submitted and e-mail it back to the student. The availability of voice transmission technology and webcams are making the simulation of an in-person tutoring session more realistic and viable. Tutors who teach advanced computer skills also tend to favor the online environment, as do language instructors who have access to software that allows them to record and receive audio lessons and assignments from their students.

Online tutoring is coming of age.

Tutors come from a variety of backgrounds and careers, with a large percentage being current or former teachers. Some tutors are students themselves, and others are scaling back their full-time jobs due to retirement or family obligations. The fact that you can set your own hours, rates, and meeting locations makes tutoring a popular job with parents of small children. Some tutors are doctoral candidates who are working on dissertations, others are pursuing artistic careers that are time-consuming but not immediately lucrative. An aspiring filmmaker with an aptitude for math can schedule tutoring around writing, shooting, and editing his or her first film. Some careers require jobseekers to undertake unpaid internships that leave them in need of money but unable to work during the day. Tutoring can be an attractive alternative to waiting tables or tending bar in the evenings and on weekends.

Yet, it is important to remember that tutoring is intensive work. It would be difficult for most people to find the energy to tutor around a full-time job. Working one-on-one with clients, whether they are eight or eighty, requires focus and discipline. A tutor's attention cannot wander, nor can a tutor rely on videos, written exercises, or other media to fill the time. Clients are usually paying a premium to study privately, and they expect individualized attention for the duration of their sessions. Tutors with their own children owe it to their clients to avoid interruptions and distractions. Often parents seek out a tutor because their child is testing behind grade level in a particular subject. Unlike a classroom teacher with many students to teach simultaneously, the tutor can proceed at whatever pace is appropriate for the child. Yet the tutor must find the key to unlocking learning for each student, and the reasons behind the child's poor school performance may be hard to diagnose and treat.

Essential Gear

Hoist your flag high and let it catch the wind. The first clue a potential client is going to have about your tutoring skills is from your advertising, so ensure that your Craigslist ads, fliers, business cards, and other promotional materials are strong and sharp and free of errors. Think about your audience, their needs and goals, and tailor your language accordingly. If your clients are going to be children, your pitch will need to appeal to their parents.

As a tutor you will choose whether to teach children with learning difficulties, gifted students seeking enhancement, or adults. The demand in your local area will also play a role in determining what types of clients you will find. As you would expect, demand for enhancement and test preparation are highest in affluent areas where parents have more money to devote to their children's education. Both upper-income areas and retirement communities will provide adult learners seeking to dabble in a new language or master computer programs. In such areas, you might find that private tutoring will function for you as a companion business to teaching classes at senior and community centers. If you do not live near enough potential clients, then online tutoring may be the best option for you. By making use of the Internet, you can expand your potential client base globally, although you will have to be careful about payment arrangements for clients who cannot put cash in your hand.

Becoming a tutor is one of the easiest career transitions to make. There are no certification or degree requirements unless you work for a professional tutoring organization or in the field of special education. There is no official accreditation body for tutors at the national, state, or local level. All you need to do is advertise your availability locally and begin to build up a client base and a reputation. That being said, there are quite a few questions that you should ask yourself, and preparations you should make, before you hang out your shingle and being your new career as a tutor.

You Are Here

You can begin your journey to your new tutoring career from many different locales.

Do you have a skill, and can you teach it? These are related, but not identical questions. Some people excel at algebra or French but are not able to teach it effectively to others. Having knowledge of a subject area or skill does not equate to being a good teacher of it, so be certain that you ask yourself these two questions separately.

Are you, by any chance, good at mathematics? High school mathematics—including algebra, geometry and trigonometry—consistently ranks as the most in-demand subject for outside tutoring. This parallels an ongoing need for math teachers in the schools, especially at middle and secondary school grade levels. There are lots of subjects you could tutor, though, so do not be put off this career path if math is not your thing. (Obviously, you are not alone!)

Do you have a lot of patience? Teaching, whether in a classroom setting or one-on-one, is immensely gratifying, but it can also be frustrating. As a tutor, you may be working with students who are behind their peers in a given subject due to learning problems, lack of motivation, psychological issues, language barriers, or a wide variety of other causes. The parents may be uninvolved and seemingly uninterested or, what is sometimes worse, overinvolved and overbearing.

Tutors must advertise for work.

Parents may hold you accountable for their offspring's lack of progress, even if said offspring shows up late, unprepared, and refusing to unplug headphones. Patience is also required to establish yourself in your new career. You will need to advertise your services and build up a base of clients. Dealing with bounced checks and cancellations can be stressful when your livelihood depends upon a steady stream of paying customers.

Organizing Your Expedition

Before you set out, know where you are going.

Decide on a destination. Your tutoring port of call will depend upon your subject area, availability, income expectations, and location. Consider first whether you want to tutor on your own or for an organization or company. As a freelancer, you are responsible for obtaining your own clients, setting your own rates, and collecting your fees. A tutoring center will take care of all the advertising and administrative tasks, leaving you free to just show up and teach. The catch is that you may need to follow their prescribed curriculum and use their proprietary textbooks or teaching methodology, and you may need to hold specific credentials or pass competency exams in your subject area in order to get hired. You might also have to tutor on their premises and within certain hours of operation. There are distinct advantages and disadvantages to both options: employee or freelancer. Only you can weigh how they stack up in your particular situation.

Scout the terrain. If you have decided to launch a career as a freelance tutor, you need to advertise your services in your local area. Craigslist is a good place to start, but you should also print up some fliers and post

Navigating the Terrain

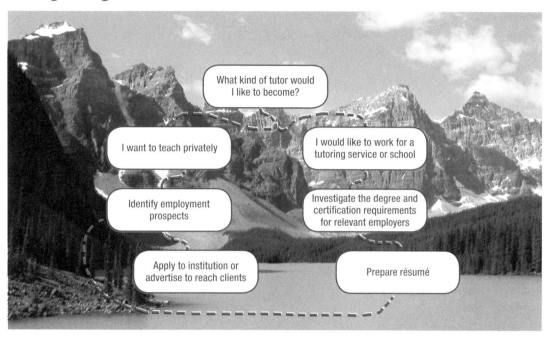

What kind of tutor would
I like to become?

I want to teach privately

I would like to work for a
tutoring service or school

Identify employment
prospects

Investigate the degree and
certification requirements
for relevant employers

Apply to institution or
advertise to reach clients

Prepare résumé

them on bulletin boards around town. Libraries, community and senior centers, bookstores, and schools, including colleges and universities (if they allow it), are likely spots for bulletin boards that will be read by prospective clients. Municipal sports facilities, houses of worship, and local newspapers are other good places to advertise your expertise. If you intend to tutor online, be sure that you have an interactive Web site that demonstrates how you will teach effectively online. A final word of advice is to speak with the guidance counselors at local schools to see how you can connect with parents who might be willing to pay for tutoring for their child.

Find the path that's right for you. If soliciting your own clients seems intimidating at this stage, do not worry. You might be better suited to working for a tutoring center. The next step for you is finding an employer who is either in your area or who offers distance learning services. Some links at the end of this chapter will get you started, but you can also search the Internet or check your local phone book. Just bear

Notes from the Field

Karen Houck
Tutor, certified educational therapist
San Francisco, California

What were you doing before you decided to change careers?

I taught full-time at a private college preparatory school for over 35 years, teaching regular high school classes for foreign students and tutoring in the Learning Support Program when it was developed. I also briefly served as principal of the school.

Why did you change your career?

I was thinking about retiring from full-time teaching, and I wanted some work that I could do part-time in my home. I had been interested in learning disabilities for some years. I found that UC Berkeley Extension had a program in educational therapy that was convenient for me, and I investigated the field a little. I discovered I was very interested in it, so I pursued it and became a Certified Educational Therapist.

in mind that a tutoring center, whether it specializes in test prep, foreign languages, or remedial math, is going to have to prove to its potential clients that its tutors are qualified, so be prepared to pony up the credentials.

Go back to school. Returning to school is rarely necessary or advisable for this career path, but there may be circumstances in which it makes sense. Since tutors usually work part-time, they are sometimes already students who need a job with flexible hours to work around their studies. Computer science majors can often find part-time jobs teaching basic computer skills, or tutoring clients who wish to learn specific programs or how to edit videos or design Web pages. Tutors who work within the school system, especially in remedial or special education, may be required to hold state teaching certification. Acquiring appropriate teaching credentials may involve returning to school, which may be worthwhile if you are considering a teaching career beyond the realm of private tutoring. If you return to school just to tutor, you are unlikely to see a financial

How did you make the transition?

I spent about three years taking courses and doing an internship before getting my certification. As soon as I had my certificate, I began doing psycho-educational assessments occasionally, and I also became co-director of the Learning Support Program at school. I've been doing a lot of networking with professionals at other schools and trying to build a reputation as someone who is competent and knowledgeable. I'm getting a reputation as the person to call with questions about disability accommodations on College Board tests. I'm taking a long time with the transition. Next year, I'll be half time at my school, and I'll try to build my private practice.

What are the keys to success in your new career?

I think the keys to success are being very competent in the field, keeping up with new developments, networking, being good at diagnosis, and building a practice by getting referrals from satisfied clients and professionals. I don't know of any magic shortcuts. If I did, I'd use them.

return on your investment, but that may not be relevant if you have other business or family demands that make a permanent part-time career your long-term goal.

Landmarks

If you are in your twenties... You might find tutoring an ideal part-time job as you complete your undergraduate or graduate degree. Test prep companies like Kaplan are eager to hire tutors who have recent high scores on the SAT, GRE, MCAT, LSAT, and other standardized tests. But putting up fliers or posting a Craigslist ad may be sufficient to garner as many clients as you can handle. Establish a good reputation by word of mouth, and you may be able to look forward to a summer free of, "May I take your order?"

If you are in your thirties or forties... It is possible that you may have small children or elderly parents to care for, and you may be looking for a flexible part-time job that will work around the needs of your family. If you are already a teacher, cutting back to part-time hours and tutoring may give you the time flexibility that you require at this stage of your life, although you may lose needed benefits.

If you are in your fifties... You might be considering early retirement but still need some income to make ends meet. Or perhaps you just want to stay active in your field or satisfy a long-held desire to teach. Beginning to tutor in the evenings and on the weekends can be a way to test the waters of your new career. You can get a sense of how well-suited you are to the work, and how much income you can expect, before you hoist anchor and set sail from your current employment.

Essential Gear

Book early for the best deals. Before you venture in search of your first client, you need to decide what to charge, and what forms of payment you will accept. The first step is to get an idea of the going rate for tutoring in your discipline in your locale. Be wary of charging too little or agreeing to travel too far to meet a client. Value your time carefully, and consider your commuting expenses if you are not tutoring in your home. If you accept checks, be prepared to confront clients when they bounce. Think about offering discounts to clients who pay in advance for a number of tutoring sessions. Such arrangements can help you plan both your time and budget.

If you are over sixty... Tutoring can be a great way for you to ease into retirement by working part-time and setting your own hours. It can also be a method of keeping your mind sharp and your skills fresh. Older clients may appreciate being taught by someone closer to their age.

Further Resources

Kaplan began by providing test preparation programs for both undergraduate and graduate school entrance exams but has now expanded its services to offer tutoring in a variety of subjects at the K–12 levels, and English language skills. http://www.kaplan.com

Kumon is a Japanese after-school tutoring program that assists children in reading and math. Like Kaplan, Kumon tutors must be trained in, and use, their proprietary teaching methods and textbooks. More than 80 percent of Kumon students are Asian. The Kumon method is well known in Asian households but virtually unheard of outside Asian circles. http://www.kumon.com

Sylvan Learning Centers offer tutoring in reading, writing, math, and SAT/ACT test preparation for grades K–12.
http://tutoring.sylvanlearning.com

Huntington Learning Centers like Sylvan, offer tutoring in reading, writing, math, and SAT/ACT test preparation for grades K–12.
http://www.huntingtonlearning.com

SMARTHINKING is an online tutoring service that contracts with colleges and universities to provide tutoring in writing and other academic subjects. Tutors, who work from home and live all over the world, must have at least a master's degree in their discipline.
http://www.smarthinking.com

Public or Private School Administrator

Public or Private School Administrator

Career Compasses

Get your bearings on what it takes to be a successful public or private school administrator.

Relevant Knowledge of school administration procedures and contacts (30%)

Caring about your school's funding, performance, and rank (20%)

Organizational Skills to juggle multiple commitments and manage numerous projects (20%)

Communication Skills to build and maintain relationships with students, teachers, parents, and other administrators (30%)

Destination: Public or Private School Administrator

Teachers may be the face of public and private school education at the K-12 level, but, at each school, many administrators are working behind the scenes to provide everything from the students to the chalk. The administrative structure of schools varies by size, budget, student demographics, and whether it is a public or private school. All schools have a principal, who oversees all administrative functions, but some schools may have one or more assistant principals, and employees, or even whole

47

departments, to manage admissions, registration, human resources, faculty oversight and evaluation, curriculum development, facilities management, and a variety of other services. If you are interested in educational administration, it is likely that you already have some interaction with your local schools. Perhaps you are a teacher, serve on the school board or PTA, or have worked with youth as a counselor or in another capacity. There are a variety of ways that you can segue into your new career, and different roles that you could take in your new field.

Essential Gear

Don't leave your dedication under the bed. The biggest difference between an effective and an ineffective school administrator is dedication. An administrator needs to care about the students, the faculty, and the performance of the school. It is not a job where you can show up at 9 A.M., leave at 5 P.M., and just go through the motions. Nothing positive happens in a school unless the administration makes it happen.

School superintendents are the top executives in the realm of educational administration. They are akin to corporate CEOs and may have similar credentials, perhaps with a sprinkling of political connections and a history of school board involvement. They are highly paid, visible administrators. In most districts, particularly urban ones, the superintendent is a political appointment or elected position. It is always a political job, and you must be politically savvy and connected at the local level to gain such a position. Slightly lower down on the totem pole are the rest of the public school district administrators, who may set policy, control hiring, or manage resources for the schools in their district; how much is centralized, and how much is left up to the individual school varies considerably by state and locality. At the school level, principals are on top, followed by one or more assistant principals. Principals oversee every aspect of running their schools. They usually work year round, unlike teachers, who follow an academic calendar. The recent trend has been for control of school policies to be shifted down from state or district control to the level of the individual school, giving principals more autonomy in setting policies and developing curricula and other guidelines for their individual schools. But this trend has been counteracted by an increase in federal legislation, such as the No Child Left Behind Act of 2001 (Public Law #107-110), which is designed to improve the performance of primary, middle, and secondary schools by establishing national standards for each grade level. In fact, the actual standards are left up to each state, as are determinations of teacher quality, but continued federal funding is dependent upon student performance in standardized tests administered by each state. Private school students are exempt from these tests, and private school administrators are free to develop their own, school-specific standards.

A great deal of the time and energy of principals and other administrators is devoted to making sure that their students perform well on multiple-choice standardized tests. Standards are set at the local, state, and national level for various grade levels and skills. The results for each school are generally made public, and the principal is held accountable if the students perform poorly.

Hiring, firing, promoting, and mediating personnel issues is another duty of educational administrators. How much of this duty falls upon the principal, and how much upon subordinate administrators, depends upon the school. It is hard to generalize, since both public and private schools vary tremendously in terms of size, quality, budget, and other characteristics. Maintaining the physical plant of the

Administrators decide about the use of limited resources.

school, and making decisions about maintenance and improvements, is also the work of administrators. Much of the repair and refurbishment of schools is done in the summertime, under the supervision of principals and subordinate administrators. The work never ends, even when students are not present.

Many principals and other administrators begin their careers as teachers and move into administration. The work is quite different, and the relationship between administration and faculty can be difficult. As an administrator, you will make tough choices about how to distribute limited resources, balancing the often conflicting concerns and opinions of faculty, staff, parents, and students. Ultimately, the administration is in charge, but a successful principal must be responsive to each of these constituencies.

Increasingly schools are taking an interest in their students that goes beyond their academic achievements. Schools are taking on a quasi-parental role, picking up where parents leave off in social development, nutrition, mental and physical health care, and myriad other aspects of childhood. From providing breakfast before the school day begins to providing child care after it ends, schools are picking up the slack in the home lives of students. As the school's role in a child's life expands, so does the administrator's.

You Are Here

You can begin your journey to becoming a public or private school administrator from many different locales.

Are you currently a teacher? Many school administrators begin their careers as teachers and move into administrative work. Some begin as librarians, school counselors, or athletic coaches. Usually, a teacher with administrative ambitions and leadership qualities will apply for an open administrative position, such as department head, curriculum specialist, or assistant principal. In some cases, a teacher may be approached by the administration and offered an administrative job at the school or district level. On the whole, your best chance of segueing into educational administration starts with a successful career as a teacher.

Do you have a related degree or work experience? Aside from teaching, there are other skills and degrees that are useful for a career in educational administration. A degree or work experience in finance, for example, can be helpful in dealing with numbers and budgets. An engineering background might be appropriate for a candidate hoping to administer a school's physical plant, while a computer science degree and related job experience would be vital to working in a school's information technology office. In small school districts, just a principal or a few administrators may share a wide variety of responsibilities, but larger districts will have more highly specialized divisions of labor. Be creative in thinking about how your current career may translate to the field of educational administration.

Larger districts are more highly specialized.

Do you have extraordinary communication skills? Elementary and secondary school administration is a juggling act in which you have to balance the needs and desires (not always easy to distinguish) of the school and district administration, the faculty, the students, the parents, and the board of education. At a public school, you are also accountable to the governor, the state legislature and, indirectly, the taxpayers in your district and state. If it is news to you that you cannot please everyone then you should stop reading right now; you are far too naïve to enter this field of employment!

Navigating the Terrain

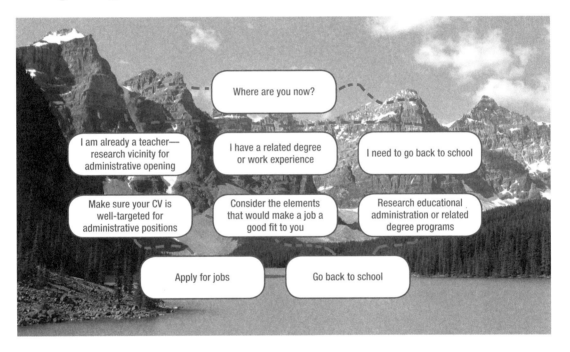

Where are you now?

I am already a teacher—research vicinity for administrative opening

I have a related degree or work experience

I need to go back to school

Make sure your CV is well-targeted for administrative positions

Consider the elements that would make a job a good fit to you

Research educational administration or related degree programs

Apply for jobs

Go back to school

Organizing Your Expedition

Before you set out, know where you are going.

Decide on a destination. If you are already a teacher, do you want to stay at your current school or at least in your current district? Or would you rather move into administration in a different school or district? Do you have a chip on your shoulder about changing the way your school is run? In what area of administration would you like to work? A larger school or district will have a greater division of labor than a smaller one, in which each administrator must wear many different hats. Think about where your talents lie, and what you enjoy and dislike about your current job. Remember that in an administrative job you will have less interaction with students and even more paperwork than in your current position.

Scout the terrain. Wherever it is you want to end up, you can begin your journey by volunteering for administrative posts within your department that are normally rotated among teachers, strengthening your relationship with the principal and other administrators, and letting them know that you are interested in an administrative post should an opening arise. If you want to move to a different school or district environment right away, use the links at the end of this chapter to find job opportunities at other schools.

Essential Gear

Pack your people skills. Educational administrators must constantly adapt to new guidelines, technologies, processes, and benchmarks. Pressure to improve student performance is applied at the district, state, and national level. Innovation is often the key to success, but it takes a savvy administrator to sell a new way of doing things to students, parents, other administrators, and the local board of education. Stellar communication skills are essential to overcoming resistance and creating excitement about new ideas and practices. Your management style can mean the difference between intransigence and enthusiasm for a given plan.

Find the path that's right for you. Of course you hope that your future administrative career is going to be fulfilling and challenging in ways that your current job is not. If you are changing careers to seek new challenges, take some time to do informational interviews with people who are in the administrative positions that interest you. Find out what they do on a day-to-day basis, the number of hours they work, the compensation they receive, and the rewards and challenges of their job. This knowledge will help you find the best way forward to a gratifying new career.

Go back to school. Some school administrators in the lowest level positions may have only a bachelor's degree, but to be eligible for promotion to even a mid-level position you will need a master's degree in educational administration; some school administrators at the higher levels even possess a Ph.D. or Ed.D. If you are a teacher, especially at secondary school level, you may already have a master's degree in education or your subject area. If you are coming from another field, such as business or finance, you probably already have a master's degree related to your current post. If you only have a bachelor's degree, you might want to start in a lower level position and see if your employer will provide tuition reimbursement for you to obtain a master's in educational administration.

Landmarks

If you are in your twenties... You might want to think about getting a master's in educational administration. If you are currently pursuing a higher degree, you might try to find an administrative job that will provide tuition reimbursement for you to finish your studies while you test the waters of educational administration. Remember that private schools generally do not require any credentials above a bachelor's degree. If you are already a teacher, look for administrative job openings and apply—you are already halfway there.

If you are in your thirties or forties... Your ability to shift smoothly into a career in educational administration will depend upon your current job situation. Start by looking for jobs that interest you, going to informational interviews, and determining if you need further education to make the switch. You might be able to parlay your existing skills and experience into a job that will eventually lead to your ideal position.

If you are in your fifties... Your first step might be to make use of personal contacts. Are you on the local school board? Do you have children in a local school? Using personal connections is a handy way to make a career transition. If you are short on academic connections, then follow

Notes from the Field

Christopher Hazeltine
Middle school dean
New York, New York

What were you doing before you decided to change careers?

I taught in a middle school in the South Bronx before deciding to become an administrator. I have an undergraduate degree in education, and it was always my plan to become a teacher.

Why did you change your career?

Deciding to become an administrator was a tough choice for me because I really enjoyed teaching. But I felt that I could better contribute to the education of students and adults if I had more responsibility to implement changes. I had a vision of what I wanted my school to look

the advice for perusing job ads, attending informational interviews, leveraging your experience, and pursuing a relevant degree.

If you are over sixty... The advice that applies to the over-fifties applies to you as well. Since teachers often move into administration after long teaching careers, age-related job discrimination may not be as acute in this area.

Further Resources

The National Association of Elementary School Principals provides advocacy, employment assistance, professional development materials and other services for elementary and middle school principals. http://www.naesp.org

The National Association of Secondary School Principals provides middle and high school principals with ideas for improving teacher and student performance, including information about national honor societies, the national student council organization, and various awards. http://www.nassp.org

like and decided to take on a role that would allow me to put my vision into action.

How did you make the transition?

Over the summer, while working for the central office as a program assistant for new teachers, I decided that it was my time to make my transition into administration. Instead of renewing my contract to teach, I applied for an open administrative position in my school.

What are the keys to success in your new career?

In order to be successful as an administrator, it is important to possess the skills needed to be a good leader, but to also remember where I came from. As a teacher prior to becoming a middle school dean, I knew what I didn't like in my administrators so I knew not to make the same mistakes.

USREAP Applications Network provides a one-stop application form for applying for teaching and administrative jobs in multiple districts. You can select as many districts as you wish, saving the time and hassle of filling out a separate application for each district and vacancy. http://www.usreap.net

Guidance Counselor or School Counselor

Guidance Counselor or School Counselor

Career Compasses

Get your bearings on what it takes to be a successful guidance counselor or school counselor.

Relevant Knowledge of issues and problems children face and, for high schools, the college admissions process (30%)

Caring about your students and their goals (10%)

Organizational Skills to keep track of all the paperwork (20%)

Communication Skills to facilitate understanding of students' concerns (40%)

Destination: Guidance Counselor or School Counselor

So you want to leave your current job and become a school counselor. Good. The need for school counselors is growing, and the availability of positions, both full- and part-time, is expected to increase. No, it is not another baby boom; it is a different educational environment, combined with a decline in the number of graduates from counseling programs. The college admissions process has become so complex, and the choices for graduating seniors so many, that more guidance counselors are

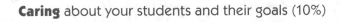

57

needed to help students navigate their options. Likewise, schools have begun to see it as their mandate to diagnose and treat the mental health and developmental problems that may keep students from working up to their potential. Counselors serve as an important liaison between teachers, students, and parents. In their own way, they can be as important and influential as teachers. Since counseling is a stressful and low-paying job, it is viewed almost as a vocation. Of course, there are exceptions. Counselors in elite private schools who are expected to get their charges into the Ivy League are well compensated for their work. The pressure on that select group of counselors is high, however: Like coaches of major sports teams, they may be fired if they do not produce results. Unlike sports managers, they do not get to choose their players. They must work with the students who attend the school and who seek out (or more likely, whose parents seek out) their services. But let us not waste too much space talking about elite private school counselors. They are only one small segment of the field. Let us consider, instead, the different types of counselor that you could become.

Essential Gear

Your degree is your passport to your new career. As this chapter has emphasized, counseling is a career with stringent educational, training, certification, and licensing requirements. They are continually changing, and they vary by job and state. The first thing a prospective employer will look at is your formal credentials. If you do not have them on paper, you will not get a chance to prove your aptitude for the job. So, make sure that you look good on paper before you apply for your first position. You can enhance your skills on the job, and continue your education, but you need certain basic qualifications just to get your foot in the door.

The work of a school counselor depends upon the grade level of the students served. Counselors at the elementary school level spend more time observing students in the classroom and evaluating their academic and developmental strengths and weaknesses than counselors of middle and secondary students. They work closely with both teachers and parents to tailor the curriculum appropriately to each student's abilities. If a student has problems of an academic or social nature, they are usually diagnosed at this stage, and the counselor directs the student's family to services that address their child's special needs. Students with disciplinary problems are sometimes directed to the school counselor rather than being punished, on the theory that at this age behavioral issues can be due to undiagnosed learning disabilities or problems at home. Counselors are needed most when students face serious crises, as in the case of violence or death among the student population.

High school counselors serve the critical role of advising students about further education and career training. They help students evaluate their educational and career ambitions in light of their academic record, and direct them toward realistic options. This process may include aptitude tests and other assessments of the students' talents and interests. Vocational counselors help the non-college-bound find their way into trade and technical schools. High school counselors often work closely with college-bound students to help them select schools that are strong in their preferred major, and they assist in navigating the admissions and financial aid process. Some counselors even help students with career placement, teaching résumé and letter-writing skills and providing information on internship and job opportunities. Guidance counselors may be responsible for organizing career fairs and coordinating visits from college admissions personnel. Counselors sometimes accompany groups of students to college fairs and arrange informational visits from financial aid and other representatives. In some schools, they are expected to wheel and deal on the telephone, advocating for their charges in the admissions and placement lottery.

A good counselor knows how to work the phone.

Counselors at all grade levels are expected to work with students individually, and to identify problems with drug or alcohol abuse and other self-destructive habits. Counselors may work with pregnant students, emancipated minors who live apart from their families, or students facing other personal challenges. Appropriate, caring, and timely intervention by a counselor can mean the difference between a student who graduates and one who drops out, between a student who goes to college and a student who winds up in jail. Often, the number of counselors is least where the need is highest, and counselors in poorer school districts may be unable to give as much individual attention to students as they would like. Some counselors have access to mental health professionals, social workers, and a variety of services for students with special needs. Counselors are not usually psychologists themselves, and their profession is distinct from school psychologists; however, these roles are sometimes combined, and a background in psychology or social work is ideal. It must be noted that, in some cases, counselors face indifferent or hostile parents and teachers and a meager budget. It really depends upon where you work. The job of counselor varies considerably by grade level and type of school.

The work environment for school counselors usually consists of an office, whose size and amenities will depend upon the affluence of the school and the priority it places on counseling. Elementary school counselors may have a play area for working with young charges, and they may spend more time observing out in the playground and the classroom. Guidance counselors may have extra space for college and career information, and may even have access to classroom space for administering tests and conducting workshops. Some counselors have support staff, others are on their own. It is a good idea to ask what kind of administrative and institutional support you will get before you accept any job.

School counselors usually follow the same academic schedule as teachers, with the caveat that they may travel to conferences, some of which take place when school is not in session. High school counselors work extremely long hours during the college admissions season.

You Are Here

You can begin your journey to guidance counseling from many different locales.

Do you have a background in psychology, social work, or another relevant field? Although education, training, and certification requirements will vary by state and type of counseling job, certain generalizations can be made. Most counselors will be expected to have a master's degree and some clinical work experience. If you have a bachelor's or master's degree in a related field, such as health sciences, education, or social work, or related work experience, you may find it easier to make the transition into your new field. If you are close to being certifiable (pun intended), you may be able to get a preliminary counseling position that provides tuition reimbursement for you to complete relevant coursework needed for licensure in your state. Teaching experience is especially helpful because most states require counselors to hold both counseling and teaching licenses.

Do you have a lot of stamina? Counseling demands endurance and the ability to compartmentalize your professional and personal lives. Each student requires your full attention and energy, and your job may put you in the position of seeing students with problems that you will find heartbreaking. Counselors need to find within themselves the ability to care without getting dragged down. The burnout rate for counselors is not as high as for social workers, but the career paths share similar forms of stress. You will not be able to save everyone. Can you live with that, or will it eat you alive? You need to give that some thought before you make the leap to change careers.

Are you up for continuing your education...and continuing...and continuing it? As more states require schools to employ counselors, the job opportunities will increase, but stringent oversight means that counselors must complete 100 hours of continuing education every five years in order to maintain their state licenses. Some counselors also have to retake certification exams, attend conferences or conventions, and keep up with the latest research in their field.

Navigating the Terrain

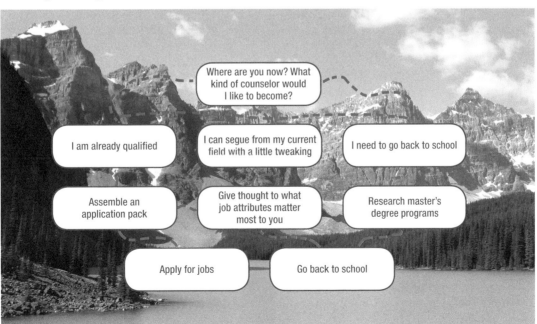

Organizing Your Expedition

Before you set out, know where you are going.

Decide on a destination. Do you like working with small children, adolescents, or young adults about to leave the school system? Do you want to help privileged youth get into college or assist the underprivileged in finding their way in the world? Would you like to work with students who have special academic needs, or behavioral and developmental problems, or would you rather focus on substance abuse, teen pregnancy, family issues, or immigration and language barriers? Would you prefer to work in an urban, rural, or suburban setting? Jobs in the suburbs are harder to come by, and demand for counselors is highest in urban areas. Consider your interests and your geographic flexibility as you begin your journey to your new career.

Essential Gear

Pack your steamer trunk with Kleenex. A thick skin and a warm heart are not always found in the same body, but both traits will help you navigate the hostile waters of your new field. Students with issues may act out in your office, blaming you for putting them in special education classes, requiring them to see specialists, or calling them to account for their grades or behavior in front of their parents. Parents may take out their disappointment on you if their offspring do not get into the college of their choice, if their test scores are low, or even if their children are put into remedial classes for their own good.

Scout the terrain. Starting with the links at the end of this chapter, investigate which jobs are available in your chosen area, and take a shrewd look at the qualifications for those jobs. Your background may provide you with some relevant expertise. A career in a health-related field, especially psychology, could help you land your first job. If you need to go back to school, find out what sort of certification courses are available in your area. Which local schools have a good track record in placing students in real jobs? Do you live in an area with a large immigrant population? If so, you may find that demand for bilingual counselors is high in your local school system.

Find the path that's right for you. As you have seen, there are many types of school counseling jobs, and picking one requires asking yourself some hard questions. Consider, above all, your financial situation. Can you afford to go back to school full-time to acquire a counseling degree?

Counseling work does not usually pay well. Is moving to be near an accredited school a realistic option for you and, if you have one, your family? Counseling is a fairly low-paying field, and the work is often stressful and can involve long hours. Can you cope with that on a long-term basis? What if you do not like your new career? The answers to these questions will help you set out on the right path.

Go back to school. Unless you are moving into counseling from a closely related field, you will need to return to school for a master's degree in counseling. Many schools will also accept a master's degree in social work (MSW), a more widely known degree. Counseling courses are usually offered in the education or psychology departments of accredited universities. Some programs can be completed part-time while you maintain your current job. To earn your license, you will probably have to complete a certain number of hours of supervised clinical or field work, much of which is unpaid. This can present a formidable barrier, depending upon your financial situation.

Landmarks

If you are in your twenties... You should think about going straight into a master's program. If you are still an undergraduate, then you can pick a relevant major, such as education or psychology. If your financial situation allows, you may be able to live at home with your parents while you finish the required hours of clinical experience.

If you are in your thirties or forties... You might want to investigate online or part-time master's programs. If you are settled and not flexible about moving, peruse job ads in your area before you embark on a course of study. Ask for informational interviews with counselors in your local schools and find out exactly what you need to do to make the transition.

If you are in your fifties... You may be ready for a big change in your life. If the kids are grown and the mortgage is paid, why not go back to

Notes from the Field

Chantell McNulty
Middle school counselor
Atlanta, Georgia

What were you doing before you decided to change careers?

I had an undergraduate degree in psychology and an MSW and worked as a probation officer in Ohio.

Why did you change your career?

I'd stayed in Ohio after graduation, but I wanted to return to Atlanta. I didn't want to continue being a probation officer so I looked for other jobs that I was qualified for.

How did you make the transition?

I just applied and got the job. I was able to start working right away, but I had to get licensed in Georgia within a certain period of time.

What are the keys to success in your new career?

You've got to love children, and working with children.

graduate school? Before you embark, it is important to remember that counseling, like social work, is a fairly low-paying field. Down-shifting from a long-term career, especially a lucrative one, to counseling can be a bumpy ride if you are not prepared for it financially. Make sure that whatever financial resources you will need for the future, such as pensions, IRAs, and life insurance, are in place before you disembark from your current job.

If you are over sixty... The first question you need to ask yourself is, "Can I relate to young people today?" Next, ask yourself if you have the emotional and physical energy to get involved in the problems of young people, many of whom suffer from self-absorption and lack of perspective, without growing bitter and cynical. If you think you have what it takes, then follow the links at the end of the chapter for information on accredited master's programs.

Further Resources

American School Counselor Association   supplies professional development materials and other resources for school counselors. http://www.schoolcounselor.org

American Counseling Association   provides information and publications for all types of counselors, not just education counselors. Their Web site contains information on accredited counseling programs. http://www.counseling.org

National Board for Certified Counselors, Inc.   lists certification requirements for all types of counselors. http://www.nbcc.org

USREAP Applications Network   provides a one-stop application form for applying for teaching and administrative jobs in multiple districts. You can select as many districts as you wish, saving the time and hassle of filling out a separate application for each district and vacancy. http://www.usreap.net

University Administrator

University Administrator

Career Compasses

Get your bearings on what it takes to be a successful university administrator.

Relevant Knowledge of educational administration procedures and contacts (30%)

Caring about your school's funding, performance, and rank (25%)

Organizational Skills to juggle multiple commitments and manage numerous projects (20%)

Communication Skills to develop and maintain relationships with students, parents, faculty, and donors (25%)

Destination: University Administrator

If you are a current faculty member looking at a career as a university administrator, you may have complicated feelings about this potential career change. The relationship between faculty and administration at both public and private colleges and universities has always been prickly and seems to be getting worse as universities move toward a corporate model of management. During the 1980s, a temporary dip in the birthrate resulted in more competition for fewer students, and at the same time states began to reduce funding for public higher education—a trend that continues today, to the frustration of public university administrators. With an eye toward cutting costs, schools began to reduce the number of tenure-track positions offered and rely on adjuncts (and, at larger research universities, graduate assistants) to teach courses, especially introductory and lower-level classes. Today, more than 50 percent of college courses are taught by adjuncts—the temps of the academic world. One result of this trend has been a movement among faculty and graduate assistants to unionize and fight for benefits, pay raises, and job security. Another result has been a severe erosion of faculty governance. What does this mean? Well, faculty used to participate in decision making, alongside administrators, through committees and other channels. With the reduction in tenured faculty has come a commensurate decrease in faculty influence on university governance. Universities are typically managed these days in a top-down style, leaving faculty members frustrated, resentful, and prone to strike. Anyone who has been privy to the posts on the average faculty mailing list in recent decades might think twice before crossing to the other side of the divide, and anyone considering a career as an administrator should be prepared. The atmosphere between the faculty and the administration on the typical college campus is Us versus Them. This is not an exhortation to avoid university administration as a career, but a warning to go into the field with your eyes open.

Essential Gear

Don't leave your dedication under the bed. The difference between an effective and an ineffective university administrator is dedication. An administrator really needs to care about the students, the faculty, and the performance of the school. It is not a job where you can show up at 9 A.M., leave at 5 P.M., and just go through the motions.

If that cold reality does not put you off, then you might want to hear more about the types of jobs that are available in university administration. The usual disclaimer applies: Jobs will vary with the size and mandate of the institution, and its status as public or private. In general, every school has an admissions office, staffed by personnel who oversee the admissions process for applicants. Every school has a financial aid office, run by administrators with the requisite background in finance. A registrar's office oversees the issuing of grades, and a residential life office deals with student housing. An office of student affairs may administer a variety of projects for students, beginning with orientation, and a career services office will help with job placement and graduate school applications. Universities duplicate most of the above offices specifically for graduate students, and they may also have offices that advise both students and faculty in the process of seeking grants and fellowships.

One key area of university administration is managing money. Colleges and universities rely on a variety of sources for their income. Tuition and fees paid by students form an increasingly large segment of this income. Endowments cover much of the remainder, with state and private funding bringing up the rear. All schools employ administrators to solicit funds from alumni and large corporate sponsors, a function that is euphemistically called "development." Anyone with a background in fund-raising or grant writing, especially for the nonprofit sector, is well-placed to get a job in development.

A school depends on many outside populations.

Another key area of university administration is public relations. Universities want the world—and potential donors—to know about the accomplishments of their faculty and alumni. They publish newsletters and magazines and generate news releases to inform media outlets and award-granting bodies of their work. This is especially true of large research universities.

Large research universities are practically towns unto themselves, with populations exceeding 30,000 in some cases. The complicated ecosystem of a university depends on many administrators with a myriad of talents—there is bound to be a place in the hierarchy for you.

You Are Here

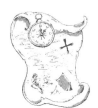

You can begin your journey to university administrating from many different locales.

Are you currently a professor? Most university administrators begin their careers as professors and move into administrative work. Departments draw from their professorial ranks for rotating positions such as graduate program director (GPD) and department chair. Professors are usually tapped when a vacancy arises for a faculty or academic dean, provost, or other position in academic affairs. On the whole, your best chance of moving into university administration is to begin as a professor.

Do you have a related degree or work experience? If you are not a professor, do not lose heart. Some positions in university administration are better filled by people with backgrounds in business. Financial aid administrators, for example, are rarely former professors, and the managers of the physical plant and information technology services sector are more likely to come from an engineering and computer science background, respectively, than a purely academic one. Athletic directors can be former coaches, but they can also come from the world of sports management, and counseling and health services are usually run by specialists in those fields. Campus food services may be overseen by administrators with degrees in hotel management, and campus safety by former police officers and even former military personnel.

Essential Gear

Pack your people skills. People naturally resist change, but university administrators must constantly adapt to new guidelines, technologies, processes, and benchmarks. Pressure to improve student performance, increase alumni contributions, and attract top faculty and research money is applied at the department, school, and even state level. Innovation is often the key to success, but it takes a savvy administrator to sell a new way of doing things to students, parents, other administrators, and faculty. Stellar communication skills are essential to overcome resistance and create excitement about new ideas and practices. Your management style can mean the difference between intransigence and enthusiasm for a given plan.

Do you have extraordinary communication skills? University administration is a juggling act in which you have to balance the concerns of the administration, the faculty, the students, parents, donors, and trustees. At a public college or university, you are also accountable to the governor, the state legislature and, indirectly, the taxpayers. If it's news to you that you cannot please everyone, then you should stop reading right now; you are far too naïve to enter this field of employment!

Navigating the Terrain

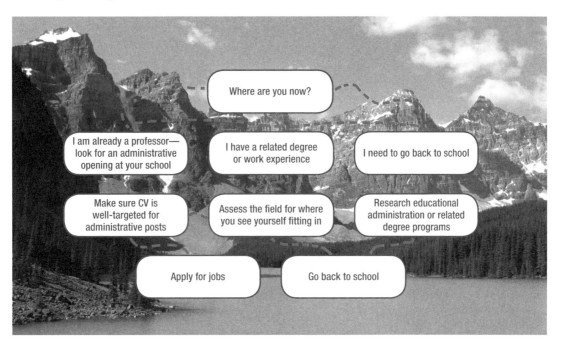

Where are you now?

I am already a professor—look for an administrative opening at your school

I have a related degree or work experience

I need to go back to school

Make sure CV is well-targeted for administrative posts

Assess the field for where you see yourself fitting in

Research educational administration or related degree programs

Apply for jobs

Go back to school

Organizing Your Expedition

Before you set out, know where you are going.

Decide on a destination. If you are already a professor, do you want to stay at your current college or university, or would you rather move into administration in a different school or geographic area? Do you have rigid opinions about changing the way your school is run? In what area of administration would you like to work? A faculty dean has different duties than someone working in residential life or admissions. Think about where your talents lie, and what you enjoy and dislike about your current job. Remember that an administrative job is going to have considerably less interaction with students and even more paperwork than your current position.

Scout the terrain. Wherever it is you want to end up, you can begin your journey by volunteering for administrative posts within your department

Notes from the Field

Erin Donnally Drake
University administrator
Amherst, Massachusetts

What were you doing before you decided to change careers?

Before I changed careers, I was in a graduate program in political science. I'd been interested in politics for a long time, and did some work as an activist. So I thought I'd try the academic side of things and go back to school.

Why did you change your career?

At my undergraduate institution, I had a tough decision as to whether or not I wanted to pursue my higher degree in higher education or in political science. I chose political science thinking that I would want to be a professor and possibly work at a think tank. I really struggled with graduate school—not with classes, but just with the feeling that I was not in the right program. Most of my classes I did actually enjoy, but I knew that I didn't want to be a professor, but I did want to stay in higher education. I was really unhappy and decided something needed to change and that ended up being a change in career path.

How did you make the transition?

When I made the decision to change career paths, I was still in the Ph.D. program in political science. I had already spent over a year in the program and knew that if I lasted two years, I would be able to leave with a master's degree. In order to transition to my new career, I knew I needed to get some experience working as a student affairs administrator. I used my contacts who already worked in higher education, and one of them knew a professor at the University of Massachusetts in the education department. I contacted him and he directed me to the

that are normally rotated among faculty, strengthening your relationship with the dean and other administrators, and generally letting it be known that you are interested in an administrative post should an opening arise. If you want to move to a different college or university environment right away, use the links at the end of this chapter to find job opportunities at other schools.

vice chancellor for student affairs here at UMass. I met with him and told him my story and how I was interested in changing fields. I told him that I didn't need a paid position, but that I just needed experience. He asked me where I wanted to work and I chose student activities. The director of the Student Activities Center interviewed me and actually offered me ten hours of paid work per week. As soon as I started working in student activities, I knew that this was my true career path. I worked really hard, and the Student Activities Center found more and more projects for me and more and more hours for me to work—I went from ten to 20 to 30 hours per week. After a year working 30 hours per week, a position opened in the office and I got the job. Over the past three years, I have been promoted and am now beginning to look for a move to another university within the next two years.

What are the keys to success in your new career?

The keys to success in my new career are hard work, pursuing varied experience, and making contacts throughout student affairs at UMass and across the country. In student affairs many administrators have multiple responsibilities, which causes busy days and often long hours. Additionally, work in Student Activities is often an evening and weekend job. When working in student affairs, one needs varied experiences in order to move up in the field. Lower positions in student affairs are very specialized, but as one moves up, one holds responsibility for more departments and must have experience in each area. While working in student activities I must get experience on committees for orientation, residence life, and other areas in order to learn about them and understand the challenges and opportunities in each. Finally, getting a job in student affairs is often about who you know. Going to conferences and meeting administrators from around the country is important for success in the field and for moving around and up in the field.

Find the path that's right for you. Of course you hope that your future administrative career is going to be fulfilling and challenging in ways that your current job is not. If you are changing careers to seek new challenges, take some time to do informational interviews with people who are in the administrative positions that interest you. Find out what they do on a day-to-day basis, the hours they work, the compensation they receive, and the rewards and challenges of their job. This knowledge will help you find the best way forward to a gratifying new career.

Go back to school. Some university administrators in the lowest level positions may have only a bachelor's degree, but you will not be eligible for promotion to even a mid-level position without a master's, and most university administrators at the higher levels possess a doctorate. If you are a professor, you probably already have a doctoral degree. If you are coming from another field, such as business or finance, you probably already have a master's related to your current position. If you only have a bachelor's degree, you might want to get a lower-level position and see if your employer will provide tuition reimbursement for you to obtain a master's.

Landmarks

If you are in your twenties... You might want to think about getting a master's in educational administration. If you are currently pursuing a higher degree, then try to find an administrative job on campus that might provide tuition reimbursement for you to finish your current studies while you test the waters of university administration.

If you are in your thirties... Your ability to shift smoothly into a career in university administration will depend upon your current employment situation. Start by looking for jobs that interest you and going to informational interviews, then determine if you need further education to make the switch. You might be able to parlay your existing skills and experience into a job that is a stepping-stone to your ideal position.

If you are in your fifties... Your first step might be to make use of personal contacts. Are you on any boards? Have you contributed to any schools, such as your alma mater? Using personal connections is a good way to make a career transition. If you are short on academic connections, then follow the advice for perusing job ads, attending informational interviews, leveraging your experience, and pursuing a relevant degree.

If you are over sixty... The advice that applies to the over-fifties applies to you as well. Since full professors often move into administration after long teaching careers, age-related job discrimination may not be as acute in this area.

Further Resources

The American Association of Collegiate Registrars and Admissions Officers is a membership organization of admissions, registration, and enrollment professionals. http://www.aacrao.org

The National Association of Student Personnel Administrators provides information on graduate programs and professional development for administrators. The Web site features a jobs board where you can post your résumé and look at vacancies. http://www.naspa.org

American Association of University Administrators is a professional networking organization. It hosts a professional development program and holds an annual conference. http://www.aaua.org

National Association of Student Financial Aid Administrators is a membership organization for financial aid personnel. Its mission is to increase financial aid opportunities so that all students who aspire to attend college can do so. Its Web site provides up-to-date news and legislative information, and career training resources. http://www.nasfaa.org/Home.asp

Language Teacher or ESL Teacher

Language Teacher or ESL Teacher

Career Compasses

Get your bearings on what it takes to be a successful language/ESL teacher.

Relevant Knowledge of English grammar and teaching methodologies (30%)

Caring about your students and their development (20%)

Organizational Skills to plan lessons and keep records for multiple classes (20%)

Communication Skills to reach students who do not understand English (30%)

Destination: Language Teacher or ESL Teacher

The life of the intrepid explorer who teaches English as a Second Language (ESL) can be both personally and professionally rewarding. It can also afford the opportunity to go on some literal journeys: English teachers can opt to teach in language schools abroad or work as private language tutors virtually anywhere in the world. The portability of this skill is part of its appeal to those with a taste for adventure. Another attractive aspect of this career is its accessibility. If you are a native speaker of English, you are already quite far along the way. Other rewards for English teachers include flexible schedules, school breaks off from work, and a feeling that you are making a difference.

Whether you teach children or adults, you can get tremendous personal satisfaction from the progress of your students. In some cases, you will know that you helped them get scholarships or jobs that are dependent upon their ability to demonstrate English language proficiency. Foreign students who wish to attend U.S. colleges and universities are usually required to achieve a minimum score on the Test of English as a Foreign Language (TOEFL) exam. Some language schools run courses just to prepare students to surmount this barrier to entry. The ability of children, in particular, to soak up new knowledge makes their progress in acquiring a new language particularly rapid. It can be quite rewarding to see a student converse confidently as you recall that he or she did not speak a word of English when the semester commenced.

Although the path to becoming an ESL teacher is theoretically open to any native speaker, and, in areas where the need for English teachers is high, to proficient non-native speakers, there are some specific skills and credentials that will smooth the way. The expertise and certification that you will need depends upon your desired destination. If you want to set a course for being a private tutor, you do not need any formal qualifications at all. Staying this course will depend upon your ability to attract and retain

Essential Gear

Unfold your map and plot your credentials. The certification requirements will vary, depending upon where you teach. Public schools will expect state teaching accreditation. Private schools will not require accreditation but will expect to see some qualifications, such as a language degree or ESL certification. Most legitimate English language schools, at home or abroad, will insist on receiving a photocopy of your ESL or TEFL certification. Some will let this requirement slide, particularly during the summer when demand is high. While this is a usually a clue that the school may be a shady operator in other areas, it is not automatically a reason to decline a job, as long as you go in with your eyes open and enough money to get yourself home if the school proves as lax about paying you as they are about qualifications and work permits. If you decide to venture out on your own as a private tutor, having credentials will make a favorable impression on potential students.

students. Private tutoring has the advantage of being flexible—you can test the waters by scheduling students around your current job, and you can do it most anywhere that you care to drop anchor. The downside is that you need to have a substantial number of students, paying pretty high rates, to make a living on this tack. It is rare for an ESL teacher to support him- or herself from private students alone, unless he or she can tap into an unusually lucrative market of wealthy clients seeking to learn business English.

If you want to stick close to home waters, you could teach at a local language school, or in your local school system. The recent increase in immigration has led to strong demand for ESL teachers in both public and private schools, as well as community colleges, adult learning centers, and vocational schools. This demand is expected to increase, so job prospects in this field are promising. Teaching in a school is quite different from working one-on-one with private students. Keeping your focus with an individual pupil in a tutoring context requires discipline and concentration, but standing in front of a class presents demands of its own. In a school environment, you may teach several different classes over the course of the day, at varying levels. This can be exhausting, and the amount of time that you will have to devote to preparing lesson plans is substantial. If you teach children, you will need a generous amount of patience, as well as classroom management skills. Adult students pose fewer disciplinary challenges, and are usually motivated, but they often have competing demands on their time and energy, leading to slower progress. Public schools require that you obtain state teaching certification, which can be a long process and require you to return to school to obtain credits in general education as well as in English teaching specifically. The advantages to teaching in a public school include full-time job status and benefits, as well as a support network of colleagues. Private schools usually do not require formal certification, but the pay and benefits are sometimes quite a bit lower. Keep in mind that ESL teaching is not a lucrative career. Pay is highest for those with full-time jobs and those who teach business English, but most teachers work part-time and most jobs lack benefits. Opportunities for advancement are virtually nonexistent, unless you choose to segue into administration and run a language school yourself.

If it is new horizons you seek, you might consider teaching in an English language school abroad. The availability of such positions is constant, with global job listings easily accessible on the Internet. Usually you will be asked to sign a contract committing to a minimum of one semester or academic year, and transportation and housing are often provided.

Essential Gear

Pack your steamer trunk with textbooks. It seems like there are almost as many textbook options as there are fish in the sea. Familiarize yourself with the major series of ESL books on the market (such as *True to Life* from Cambridge University Press, which is geared to adult learners). Many schools will expect you to choose your own course books, so you should have an idea of which ones you like and which do not appeal to you. The approaches vary considerably, and it is no fun to use a textbook that you find to be inaccurate or poorly organized, or that simply does not suit your teaching style. While you are gathering provisions for your journey, stock up on English grammar books as well.

Teaching can be a great way to finance your world travels. In return, the language schools will often work you hard, assigning you to numerous classes per day with students of varying ages and abilities. Asia is a growing market; if you want to teach in Europe, you will find the competition for jobs fiercer, and the pay lower. European language schools often take on extra teachers in the summer, when both workers and students spend their holidays learning English. Schools that hire teachers for seasonal work are less likely to procure work visas and may reject applicants without the legal right to work in that country. Some schools will allow you to work illegally on a cash basis, but these are not likely to be the best situations.

Legitimate language schools throughout the world will require their teachers to be certified in ESL teaching. Due to the romantic allure of teaching English abroad, providing this certification is a huge business. Wherever you live, there is likely to be at least one certification program available to you. In many places, there will be dozens from which to choose. Before you pick one, take a look at some of the many job ads posted on the Internet and see what sort of certification is required where you want to teach. There are several well-respected and recognized certifications, and it is worth your while to choose courses that lead to them, even if other courses are cheaper. The length and substance, as well as the price, of certification courses vary significantly. Taking one can be a good investment but, like any investment, you need to do your research ahead of time to avoid the educational equivalent of the fleabag hotel. Remember that you do not have to take a teacher training course at home. Courses are offered in most English-speaking countries, and combining a vacation with a course is a fun way to get your credentials. The Cambridge CELTA and the Trinity Cert TESOL are the most widely recognized certifications worldwide. Equivalent courses are more common in the United States, but they are not always recognized by language schools.

Like any profession, ESL has its own lingo, and this one includes a lot of acronyms. Familiarize yourself with the most common ones so the wealth of information available to you online is not confusing. Here is a primer:

ESL: English as a Second Language (used mainly in the United States)

TESL: Teaching English as a Second Language

TESOL: Teaching English to Speakers of Other Languages

ESOL: English for Speakers of Other Languages

TEFL: Teaching English as a Foreign Language (the more common term in Europe)

ELT: English Language Teaching

EFL: English as a Foreign Language

These terms are used interchangeably, with one caveat: the terms with "F," for English as a foreign language, usually refer to students who learn English in their home country for business, travel, school, or leisure. The terms with "S," for English as a second language, refer to immigrants who are learning English in an English-speaking country.

You Are Here

You can begin your journey to ESL teaching from many different locales.

Do you speak a foreign language, or have the legal right to work in a foreign country? Although it is not necessary to speak another language to teach English, it can certainly help, especially if you want to live abroad. Living in a foreign culture can be stressful and isolating; any connection with your new home, whether through ethnicity or previous study, will ease the transition. It is also important to remember that some language schools will not provide work visas. Some will, but the legal right to work in your country of choice will be a major asset on the job market. It is possible to work "under the table," and many English teachers do so, but there is less stability with this lifestyle choice.

Do you have a related degree or work experience? Any teaching experience you have will be of benefit on your new career path; the communication and organizational skills you needed for teaching computer programming or sailing will cross over to teaching English. Performing experience is also useful, as you are "on" when in front of a class just as in front of an audience. If you were an English major in college, and have worked as an editor or writer, your English skills are likely to be above average. This knowledge will help propel you to certification and soften your landing in your new environment.

Experience as an ESL teacher will look good on your résumé if you seek other teaching jobs in the future, but may not be considered relevant in other fields. This is something you should consider before going into ESL teaching. Should you decide to change tack after working as an ESL teacher for a while, you will want to emphasize to potential employers such transferable skills as thinking on your feet, excellent grammar skills, poise and public speaking ability, patience, ability to work with diverse groups of people, and communication skills.

Do you have a lot of patience? If you have toiled in a windowless cubicle for many years, teaching English can sound like the ticket to a vacation lifestyle of fun in the sun. That may be true enough for your leisure time, but do not underestimate the demands that teaching will make on you. Have you tried to learn a foreign language? Think about how hard it was to understand the teacher and learn the grammar. You could be facing a roomful of 30 people in that frustrating position every day. Depending on your destination, you may be working with children who do not get any language reinforcement outside of school and who would rather whisper about you in their own language to their classmates. Make sure patience is the first item on your packing list—just like sunscreen, you will need a lot of it, and you will not want to run out.

Navigating the Terrain

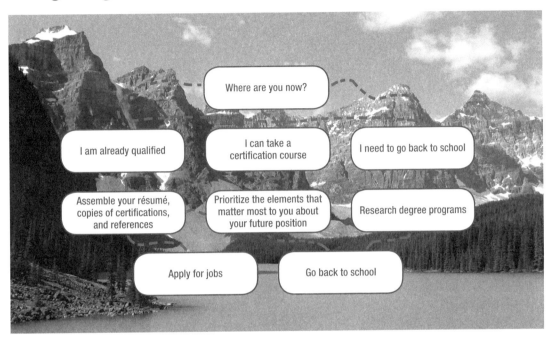

Where are you now?

I am already qualified

I can take a certification course

I need to go back to school

Assemble your résumé, copies of certifications, and references

Prioritize the elements that matter most to you about your future position

Research degree programs

Apply for jobs

Go back to school

Organizing your Expedition

Before you set out, know where you are going.

Decide on a destination. Are your sights set on exotic locales, such as Asia, or are you thinking about keeping your journey closer to home, perhaps teaching the children of immigrants? Consider carefully whether you would like to teach children or adults, as these groups demand different skill sets. You will also need to decide if the appropriate vehicle for your journey is the public school system, a private school, a community college or adult education center, or a dedicated language school. Or maybe you would like to roam freely as a private tutor. Another decision you will need to make before you take the mothballs out of your suitcases is what type of English you want to teach. Teaching business English is the most lucrative, but the environment is often corporate. Does that suit you? Do you get along with business types? Would you rather teach conversational English to tourists and retirees? Are you a grammar maven who could drill high school students on the correct use

Notes from the Field

Louise Fullmer
ESL teacher
New York, New York

What were you doing before you decided to change careers?

This was actually my second career change. I was a double music/English major in college, and had tried initially to pursue a career in opera. This proved to be difficult as there are many more talented singers than there are jobs. By my mid-twenties, I was casting about for another way to earn a living that would be meaningful to me. Since I was concerned about the environment, I initially went back to school for a master's degree in environmental policy. I worked in this field, for both nonprofit organizations and the government before I changed course and started teaching.

Why did you change your career?

I found environmental work frustrating. I wanted to make a difference, but I felt I was trapped in minutiae, pushing papers around but not really helping to prevent or remediate environmental destruction. Also, I really wanted to travel. I wanted a portable job that I could do virtually anywhere in the world. I had done some freelance writing and editing work when I was in grad school, and I knew my English skills were strong. I knew from my environmental work with organizations abroad that English language skills are often prerequisites to jobs, and demand for teachers is high. Teaching English seemed the perfect way to combine my love for travel with my need to finance my journeys.

How did you make the transition?

The first phase of the transition for me was researching English language schools in places where I wanted to live. I looked at job ads online to see what sort of qualifications and experience they required.

of the future perfect tense? How about teaching children who speak another language at home with their parents? What type of English you teach is linked to where you teach. Would you like to teach abroad or stay at home? Job opportunities, and compensation, will depend heavily upon where you live.

Luckily for me, none seemed to care if applicants had previous teaching experience, but the legit schools did require proof of certification. My next step was to take an intensive TEFL certification course. I did it full-time and got my certificate quickly. It's a good idea to line up a job in advance but, in my case, I moved to the city of my choice and applied to language schools after I arrived. I was able to cobble together enough hours between several schools, plus a few private students, but it did take some juggling to keep my schedule straight and earn enough money to survive.

What are the keys to success in your new career?

This question requires a two-part answer as there are keys to success for getting a job and for performing the job. The keys to getting an ESL teaching job are timing and qualifications. Jobs, especially in Europe, are seasonal, with the highest demand in the summer. You need to time your application so that you get a slot with the hours you want before they are overwhelmed with applications. For an academic year job, it is best to apply early as well, before they have filled their courses for the semester. The other key to getting a job is including a copy of your certification, and detailing any relevant experience that you have, with your application. If they have to ask you to send the certificate, they'll give the job to someone else. There are more applicants than jobs, so first impressions matter. But don't despair if your favored school is full up at present. Keep checking in with them, as the attrition rate is high. Once in a while schools must fill in for a teacher who has had to leave mid-session. Once you have a job, you will need to be supremely organized to keep track of multiple classes that are at different levels. You will also need to be able to think on your feet. If one exercise is not working, you need to have something else in your bag of tricks to fill the time productively. Teaching really is a performance, so perhaps I have not traveled so far from opera after all!

Scout the terrain. Starting with the links at the end of this chapter, investigate what jobs are available in your chosen area, and take a shrewd look at the qualifications for those jobs. Your background may provide you with some relevant expertise. A career in business could help you relate to the needs of students learning English for business purposes and, since business English is the best paid of the ESL options, your business acumen could help you upgrade to a first class position. What certification courses are available in your locale? Which local schools have a good track record of placing students in real jobs? Do you live in an area with a large immigrant population? If so, you may find that demand for ESL teachers is high in your local school system.

Find the path that's right for you. There are many roads to teaching English in Rome, and in all of the other compelling destinations that may lure you. Consider, above all, your financial situation. What type of certification course is within your budget? Can you afford to go back to school full-time to acquire an education degree? Is moving abroad, temporarily or permanently, a realistic option for you, and your family, if you have one? Teaching is a low-paying field and much of the work is part-time, without benefits. Do you need health insurance? Can you afford to live on part-time wages? The answers to these questions will help you set out on the right path.

Go back to school. ESL courses range from 20-hour part-time programs to 120-hour full-time intensive courses. Costs can be as low as $400 for a 20-hour, weekend course to upwards of $3,000 for a full-time course with grammar modules and practice teaching. Consider your budget, your time frame, and the certification required by your chosen destination. Before you commit to a school, inquire about the success their students have had in acquiring jobs. If you think you would like to teach in a public school, find out what courses your state requires for accreditation. Most states require that you take some general education courses in addition to specific requirements for your field of expertise. If demand for teachers is strong, as it may be in some inner-city neighborhoods with high rates of teacher attrition, public schools may let you teach on a provisional license while you build the necessary credentials.

Landmarks

If you are in your twenties... You are ideally situated for testing the waters of language teaching. If you are still in school, you can take an intensive certification course during a school break, and then spend your summers teaching in exotic locales. If you are working, you can take a part-time course and, once you are certified, you can teach locally in the evenings before taking the plunge to teach full-time. Want to try graduate school? Look for master's programs in foreign languages or ESL teaching. A formal degree can help you set sail on a lifelong career.

If you are in your thirties or forties... You need to consider what responsibilities you have accumulated on your life's adventure thus far. If you have a spouse, children, or a mortgage or other significant debts, then jetting off to join the faculty of a language school in Seoul might not be a realistic option. Luckily for you, there are plenty of teaching opportunities closer to home. Look at the immigrant profile in your community. There may be a need for ESL teachers in local public and private schools or in adult education centers and community colleges, and there may be a market for private tutors. You may not be able to teach full-time, but part-time experience can help you set sail toward a career change on the horizon.

If you are in your fifties... You may be ready for a big change in your life. If the kids are grown and the mortgage is paid off, why not see what it is like to live in Thailand? Before you embark, it is important to be aware that teaching is an extremely low-paying field. Down-shifting from a long-term career, especially a lucrative one, to teaching can be a bumpy ride if you are not prepared for it financially. Make sure that whatever financial resources you will need for the future, such as pensions, retirement accounts, and health insurance, are in place before you disembark from your current job.

If you are over sixty... You may be eligible for retirement but in the market for an adventure rather than a rest. Since teaching jobs are often part-time and on short-term contracts, you are likely to face less discrimination than you would starting out at this age in many other fields. Once you have acquired the appropriate certification for your chosen path, you will need to show potential employers that you are dynamic and can relate to younger students in the classroom. Older adult students who are learning English for leisure or travel may prefer to have a teacher whom they can relate to a bit better than a twenty-something backpacker, so you may want to focus your job hunt on language learning centers that cater to this particular student population.

Further Resources

The Center for Adult English Language Acquisition provides numerous resources for professional development for ESL teachers.
http://www.cal.org/caela

Transitions Abroad.com provides general resources for working abroad. The section on Teaching English Abroad is a treasure trove of links to useful Web sites.
http://www.transitionsabroad.com

Dave's ESL Cafe is a well-known site that provides information but also boasts a lively discussion forum frequented by ESL teachers from around the globe. Get your newbie questions answered here.
http://www.eslcafe.com

Developing Teachers.com features lesson plans and classroom resources for English language teachers at all levels.
http://developingteachers.com

Special Education Teacher

Special Education Teacher

Career Compasses

Get your bearings on what it takes to be a successful special education teacher.

Relevant Knowledge of teaching techniques for disabled students (25%)

Caring about your students' progress and quality of life (25%)

Organizational Skills to keep track of individual students and required paperwork (10%)

Communication Skills to reach students who may face a range of challenges (40%)

Destination: Special Education Teacher

What is special about special education? The term can apply to a learning environment that is adapted to the pace and needs of students with mental and physical disabilities who cannot fully function in a normal classroom setting. Special education students used to bear a stigma. A student who rode the "short bus" to school or who had to make a lonely trek down the hallway to a remedial class was often teased or ostracized.

Before Congress passed the Individuals with Disabilities Education Act (IDEA) in 1975, the drop-out rate for special education students was high, with few earning a high school degree or achieving employment and independence in their adult lives. Before the passage of this landmark piece of federal legislation, students with physical or mental handicaps were generally shut out of public education. If their parents were wealthy, they could seek private assistance, but the majority of children with special needs received no help. As recently as the 1960s, parents were encouraged to institutionalize disabled children and forget about them. This advice applied not only to children with profound physical and developmental handicaps, but even to children who would today likely be mainstreamed and go on to college and graduate school. The changes that have occurred in the last 30 years in extending public education to disabled students have been tremendous, and the job of special education teacher is one of the fastest growing educational careers.

IDEA requires public schools to provide an appropriate education for every child, regardless of disability. In practice, this means that accommodations must be made so that physically disabled students can get the same education as their able-bodied peers. These accommodations can take many forms, such as note-takers, sign language interpreters, and alternative testing formats. For students whose disabilities are mental rather than physical, appropriate accommodation can mean anything from a separate learning facility to extra tutoring that allows the student to remain in a regular classroom. In recent years, as the number of recognized disabilities has expanded exponentially and these disabilities are diagnosed in more students at younger ages; the demand for teachers who work with disabled students has grown proportionally. The educational playing field has shifted from one extreme, where disabled students were shut out, through a middle ground where they were accommodated but stigmatized, to a scenario where many children are diagnosed with disabilities of varying severity and have the right to a range of accommodations. Even gifted students are entitled to special accommodations so that they can work to a higher level at a faster pace and not be held back by their classmates.

The days when students were simply labeled as "slow learners" or "retarded" are over. Now, specific learning disabilities are pinpointed with increasing precision, so that each student has an equal chance to participate and excel. The most significant aspect of this diagnostic evolution in the landscape of special education has been the discovery that many learning disabilities are not symptomatic of a lack of native intelligence. Students who once would have languished in remedial mathematics or reading classes, for example, are now tested for dyslexia and other processing disorders, and treated for the cause of the problem (dyslexia) rather than its symptoms (an apparent weakness in math or reading). Increasingly common disabilities such as Attention Deficit Hyperactivity Disorder (ADHD) and autism are now subdivided into different levels and manifestations. There is no longer any such disability as autism per se; rather, there are a whole host of problems that fall under the category of Autism Spectrum Disorders (ASD), some of which are related to intelligence, others to social skills or motor skills. The particular issues that a given child has are identified and specific treatment prescribed, including an Individualized Education Program (IEP), which is mandated by IDEA. The treatment plan may involve child psychologists, physical therapists, speech pathologists, audiologists, and drugs, as well as special education teachers. The increasing sub-categorization of learning disabilities means that special education teachers can specialize, developing particular expertise with a given disability and age group. If you are contemplating a career in special education, you should think about the various categories of learning disabilities and which age and disorder would best match your talents and interests.

Essential Gear

Don't leave home without a generous supply of patience. Even the brightest and best-behaved children try the patience of their teachers at times, and children who have difficulty communicating, comprehending what they are asked to do, or completing tasks grow frustrated, and this frustration can manifest in ways that would try the patience of a saint. All teachers need superhuman patience just to get through an ordinary school day, but special educators are in a unique position. The usual goals and benchmarks of progress have to be set aside, and the teacher must learn to accept the student's pace of learning. A special education teacher may have to go over the same simple task with a student day after day, and the child may never master it. The usual advice when packing for a journey is to take half the clothes and twice the money you originally planned on bringing. Your wardrobe is not relevant here, but, to undertake this journey, you will need twice the patience that you now imagine that you need, and then some.

Most special education teachers are employed at elementary schools, but increasing numbers are working with secondary school children and even college students. Colleges are now accepting learning-disabled students, even high-functioning people with Down syndrome, and providing them with additional resources so that they can be educated in regular college classes and, in some cases, earn degrees. This practice is not without controversy, but you can read more about it and judge its merits for yourself. The majority of special educators work in public schools, and over half belong to teachers' unions. The median earnings of special education teachers as of May 2006 were around $47,000. As stated earlier, employment prospects are far better than average for this career. The proportion of school children who qualify for special education services is increasing steadily, and the need for special education teachers for children as young as toddlers is growing as disabilities are diagnosed earlier. Also, more children today survive birth defects, accidents, and illnesses that would have killed them generations ago, and they may be left with physical and mental impairments. You should also know that the demand for special education teachers is not distributed evenly across the country. There are more job openings in poor urban and rural schools than in suburban schools or wealthy urban areas. There are also more positions in the South and West, where the population is growing at a faster rate. These areas also have a high demand for bilingual special education teachers, and the need for Spanish-speaking educators is increasing rapidly. Most special education teachers work in schools, but a few work in residential facilities or visit homebound students.

You Are Here

You can begin your journey to special education teaching from many different locales.

Are you currently a teacher? If you are already a K–12 teacher, your voyage to the realm of special education will be smoother. Special education teachers must hold a general teaching license for their state as a base requirement and complete at least one or two years at a minimum of supervised teaching. Then they must fulfill additional requirements specifically for special education teachers. If you already hold teaching credentials, then your journey will be shortened. You will also have an advantage in the job market due to your familiarity with the local school system, and you will have some idea of how suited you are to the profession of teaching, and which age level you prefer.

Do you have a related degree or work experience? If you are not a teacher, do not give up on a career in special education. You will probably need to return to school for general education credits and graduate work in special education, but there are several fields with transferable skills and experience. If you are a mental health professional or counselor, especially one who works with children, you will have both a practical and paper advantage in your new career. The same can be said if you are a therapist, whether involved in physical therapy, speech, or even occupational or recreational therapy. Working with geriatric patients, including those who suffer from the effects of stroke and dementia, bears similarities to working with disabled children. Work as a social worker would also provide an ideal background for special education teaching.

Diverse skills are essential.

Do you possess extraordinary creativity and observation skills? All children are individuals, and no two children learn in the same way, at the same pace. A regular classroom teacher will have some students who are ahead of the class, and a few who lag behind, but they will all work from a single lesson plan. A special education teacher has no standard lesson plan. Disabled students use individualized education plans because no two students are disabled in the exact same way, and to the exact same degree. Each disability has a range of characteristics, and no two children with the same disability will have identical impairments or symptoms. Reaching each student requires not just teaching on your part, but learning what works and what does not work for each child. You will have to adapt your lessons continually, based upon the child's reaction and progress at that moment. If some technique is not working, you need to be able to come up with something else, immediately. Experience will help with this process, but creative problem-solving skills will be your passport to success.

Navigating the Terrain

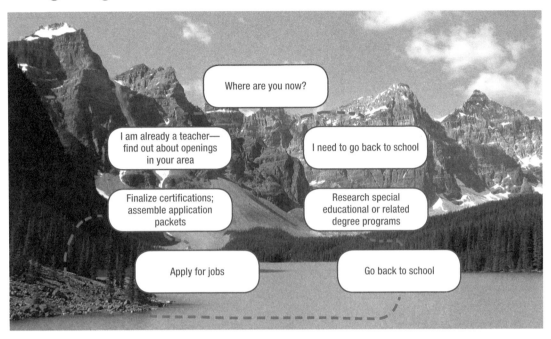

Where are you now?

I am already a teacher— find out about openings in your area

I need to go back to school

Finalize certifications; assemble application packets

Research special educational or related degree programs

Apply for jobs

Go back to school

Organizing Your Expedition

Before you set out, know where you are going.

Decide on a destination. What is motivating you to become a special education teacher? Perhaps you know a child with a disability, and you want to help children like him or her. Or maybe you just feel that you possess the special blend of patience, creativity, caring, and communication skills that this job requires. Whatever your motivation, there are a variety of destinations within your new career territory.

Scout the terrain. Unless you are immutably focused on one area of specialization, it is prudent to see where the jobs are before you make a choice. Look at advertisements for special education teachers and spot patterns. Are most jobs calling for bilingual teachers? Language skills are most in demand in large coastal cities, and in the South and

West. Are there more openings for teachers who deal with physical or mental disabilities? In most areas, it is the latter. Is there a particular age group with a higher demand? Generally, demand is growing for teacher who can work with younger children, especially infants and toddlers.

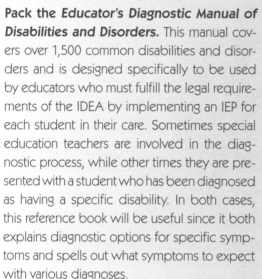

Essential Gear

Pack the *Educator's Diagnostic Manual of Disabilities and Disorders.* This manual covers over 1,500 common disabilities and disorders and is designed specifically to be used by educators who must fulfill the legal requirements of the IDEA by implementing an IEP for each student in their care. Sometimes special education teachers are involved in the diagnostic process, while other times they are presented with a student who has been diagnosed as having a specific disability. In both cases, this reference book will be useful since it both explains diagnostic options for specific symptoms and spells out what symptoms to expect with various diagnoses.

Find the path that's right for you. It is wise to gear your acquisition of new job skills to the available openings, but special education teaching is a labor of love, a vocation as much as a job, so you need to pick an area of focus that is meaningful to you and that makes use of your natural talents and the skills you have acquired in your previous career. There is a big difference between teaching basic life skills to mentally disabled children and teaching physically disabled students of normal intelligence. Some teachers work with mainstreamed students for a brief period each day in a separate classroom and others go to children's homes and work closely with them and their parents in a therapeutic manner. Only you can know which type of working environment is right for you.

Go back to school. As noted previously, even if you are a licensed teacher, you will need to go back to school to move into the field of special education. In addition to fulfilling all of the general educational requirements to obtain a standard teaching license, you will need to take additional credits in special education. In some cases, you will need to specialize in a particular disability, and most states require a one-year master's degree in special education in addition to the bachelor's degree required for mainstream classroom teaching. The licensing requirements vary by state, so you should explore the links at the end of the chapter to find out the requirements in your state. Some states require a period of supervised teaching, and some require additional assessment tests.

Landmarks

If you are in your twenties... You might want to think about getting a master's in special education straightaway. If you are currently pursuing a bachelor's degree, consider majoring in education or in a related field, such as psychology. Look first at licensing requirements in your state, and then use the resources below to find appropriate graduate programs.

If you are in your thirties or forties... Your path to your new career depends on your current job and financial situation. If you are already a teacher, then you might be able to keep your current teaching job while you pursue your master's degree in special education and gain the specialized teaching experience that you will need to obtain a license. If you are segueing from another field, you could look into part-time and distance-learning options to fulfill your educational requirements.

If you are in your fifties... Think about going back to school full-time to get your master's in special education in one year. This will give you time to plan ahead as to how you will handle your one to two years of practice teaching, and to assess job prospects in your area or in locations to which you would be prepared to move.

If you are over sixty... You can rest assured that the rising demand for special education teachers makes age-related discrimination in hiring less likely than in many other professions. Yet you should also ask yourself if you are willing and able to handle the emotional and sometimes physical toll of teaching students with disabilities.

Notes from the Field

Lois Turetsky
Special education teacher (reading)
Brooklyn, New York

What were you doing before you decided to change careers?

As an undergraduate student at Brooklyn College, I majored in educa-
tion. I taught mainstream elementary education for 12 years. I became
interested in special education after teaching the low-functioning, more
difficult children who were placed in my heterogeneous class. Reaching
the more challenged students was the most gratifying part of my job.

Why did you change your career?

I really did not change my career except for direction. As a special
education teacher, I received more gratification by the successes of the
neediest of children. While I felt that the regular and gifted classes
were as hungry for enrichment, they could succeed without the indi-
vidualized attention. Special-needs children required dedicated and in-
dividual care.

How did you make the transition?

Once my goals were established, I took a second master's in special
education. My first is in elementary education. My first classes were

Further Resources

National Center for Special Education Personnel & Related Service Providers is a career development Web site geared to career changers who are thinking of moving into special education. Yes, it Is as if it were designed just for you. http://www.personnelcenter.org

The Council for Exceptional Children is a one-stop shop for information on degree programs, financial aid, accreditation and licensure, and career services, and it features the latest research on best practices and teaching strategies. http://www.cec.sped.org

The New Teacher Center at UCSC is a career development Web site for new teachers that focuses on retention. It is not geared toward special

with emotionally challenged children in grades four and five, which had a smaller class size than mainstream classrooms, and was taught with the aid of a paraprofessional. Thereafter, I became a resource room teacher who taught reading and math as a pullout program for grades one through five. This means I worked with students who were not so academically challenged that they were entirely removed from mainstream classes. I provided extra assistance in areas in which they had trouble, helping them to keep up with their grade level.

What are the keys to success in your new career?

Compassion and patience are the keys to success in teaching the challenged student. They know what is expected of them, and they will strive to achieve the favor of their mentors when they know that their teacher is dedicated and caring. The process is time consuming and tedious, and requires a greater commitment both within and without of the school setting. Not that mainstream teaching doesn't require these qualities, but students who are academically challenged cannot thrive unless you are willing to go that extra mile for them. I often took students on trips and went home with them to see their lives outside of school. Even now I receive calls from former, grateful students.

education specifically, but the problem of teacher retention holds for this subcategory of educators as well. http://www.newteachercenter.org
National Association of Special Education Teachers   is a membership organization that provides career development and other resources to special education teachers. http://www.naset.org

Appendix A

Going Solo: Starting Your Own Business

Starting your own business can be very rewarding—not only in terms of potential financial success, but also in the pleasure derived from building something from the ground up, contributing to the community, being your own boss, and feeling reasonably in control of your fate. However, business ownership carries its own obligations—both in terms of long hours of hard work and new financial and legal responsibilities. If you succeed in growing your business, your responsibilities only increase. Many new business owners come in expecting freedom only to find themselves chained tighter to their desks than ever before. Still, many business owners find greater satisfaction in their career paths than do workers employed by others.

The Internet has also changed the playing field for small business owners, making it easier than ever before to strike out on your own. While small mom-and-pop businesses such as hairdressers and grocery stores have always been part of the economic landscape, the Internet has made reaching and marketing to a niche easier and more profitable. This has made possible a boom in *microbusinesses*. Generally, a microbusiness is considered to have under ten employees. A microbusiness is also sometimes called a *SoHo* for "small office/home office."

The following appendix is intended to explain, in general terms, the steps in launching a small business, no matter whether it is selling your Web-design services or opening a pizzeria with business partners. It will also point out some of the things you will need to bear in mind. Remember also that the particular obligations of your municipality, state, province, or country may vary, and that this is by no means a substitute for doing your own legwork. Further suggested reading is listed at the end.

Crafting a Business Plan

It has often been said that success is 1 percent inspiration and 99 percent perspiration. However, the interface between the two can often be hard to achieve. The first step to taking your idea and making it reality is constructing a viable *business plan*. The purpose of a business plan is to think things all the way through, to make sure your ideas really are profitable, and to figure out the "who, what, when, where, why, and how" of your business. It fills in the details for three areas: your goals, why you think they are attainable, and how you plan to get to there. "You need to know where you're going before you take that first step," says Drew Curtis, successful Internet entrepreneur and founder of the popular newsfilter Fark.com.

Take care in writing your business plan. Generally, these documents contain several parts: An *executive summary* stating the essence of the plan; a *market summary* explaining how a need exists for the product and service you will supply and giving an idea of potential profitability by comparing your business to similar organizations; a *company description* which includes your products and services, why you think your organization will succeed, and any special advantages you have, as well as a description of *organization* and *management*; and your *marketing and sales strategy*. This last item should include market highlights and demographic information and trends that relate to your proposal. Also include a *funding request* for the amount of start-up capital you will need. This is supported by a section on *financials*, or the sort of cash flow you can expect, based on market analysis, projection, and comparison with existing companies. Other needed information, such as personal financial history, résumés, legal documents, or pictures of your product, can be placed in *appendices*.

Use your business plan to get an idea of how much startup money is necessary and to discipline your thinking and challenge your preconceived notions before you develop your cash flow. The business plan will tell you how long it will take before you turn a profit, which in turn is linked to how long it will before you will be able to pay back investors or a bank loan—which is something that anyone supplying you with money will want to know. Even if you are planning to subside on grants or you are not planning on investment or even starting a for-profit company, the discipline imposed by the business plan is still the first step to organizing your venture.

A business plan also gives you a realistic view of your personal financial obligations. How long can you afford to live without regular income? How are you going to afford medical insurance? When will your business begin turning a profit? How much of a profit? Will you need to reinvest your profits in the business, or can you begin living off of them? Proper planning is key to success in any venture.

A final note on business plans: Take into account realistic expected profit minus realistic costs. Many small business owners begin by underestimating start-ups and variable costs (such as electricity bills), and then underpricing their product. This effectively paints them into a corner from which it is hard to make a profit. Allow for realistic market conditions on both the supply and the demand side.

Partnering Up

You should think long and hard about the decision to go into business with a partner (or partners). Whereas other people can bring needed capital, expertise, and labor to a business, they can also be liabilities. The questions you need to ask yourself are:

☞ Will this person be a full and equal partner? In other words, are they able to carry their own weight? Make a full and fair assessment of your potential partner's personality. Going into business with someone who lacks a work ethic, or prefers giving directions to working in the trenches, can be a frustrating experience.

☞ What will they contribute to the business? For instance, a partner may bring in start-up money, facilities, or equipment. However, consider if this is enough of a reason to bring them on board. You may be able to get the same advantages in another way—for instance, renting a garage rather than working out of your partner's. Likewise, doubling skill sets does not always double productivity.

☞ Do they have any liabilities? For instance, if your prospective partner has declared bankruptcy in the past, this can hurt your collective venture's ability to get credit.

☞ Will the profits be able to sustain all the partners? Many start-up ventures do not turn profits immediately, and what little they do produce can be spread thin amongst many partners. Carefully work out the math.

Also bear in mind that going into business together can put a strain on even the best personal relationships. No matter whether it is family, friends, or strangers, keep everything very professional with written agreements regarding these investments. Get everything in writing, and be clear where obligations begin and end. "It's important to go into business with the right people," says Curtis. "If you don't—if it degrades into infighting and petty bickering—it can really go south quickly."

Incorporating. . . or Not

Think long and hard about incorporating. Starting a business often requires a fairly large—and risky—financial investment, which in turn exposes you to personal liability. Furthermore, as your business grows, so does your risk. Incorporating can help you shield yourself from this liability. However, it also has disadvantages.

To begin with, incorporating is not necessary for conducting professional transactions such as obtaining bank accounts and credit. You can do this as a sole proprietor, partnership, or simply by filing a DBA ("doing business as") statement with your local court (also known as "trading as" or an "assumed business name"). The DBA is an accounting entity that facilitates commerce and keeps your business' money separate from your own. However, the DBA does not shield you from responsibility if your business fails. It is entirely possible to ruin your credit, lose your house, and have your other assets seized in the unfortunate event of bankruptcy.

The purpose of incorporating is to shield yourself from personal financial liability. In case the worst happens, only the business' assets can be taken. However, this is not always the best solution. Check your local laws: Many states have laws that prevent a creditor from seizing a non-incorporated small business' assets in case of owner bankruptcy. If you are a corporation, however, the things you use to do business that are owned by the corporation—your office equipment, computers, restaurant refrigerators, and other essential equipment—may be seized by creditors, leaving you no way to work yourself out of debt. This is why it is imperative to consult with a lawyer.

There are other areas in which being a corporation can be an advantage, such as business insurance. Depending on your business needs, insurance can be for a variety of things: malpractice, against delivery failures or spoilage, or liability against defective products or accidents. Furthermore, it is easier to hire employees, obtain credit, and buy health insurance as an organization than as an individual. However, on the downside, corporations are subject to specific and strict laws concerning management and ownership. Again, you should consult with a knowledgeable legal expert.

Among the things you should discuss with your legal expert are the advantages and disadvantages of incorporating in your jurisdiction and which type of incorporation is best for you. The laws on liability and how much of your profit will be taken away in taxes vary widely by state and country. Generally, most small businesses owners opt for *limited liability companies* (LLCs), which gives them more control and a more flexible management structure. (Another possibility is a *limited liability partnership*, or *LLP*, which is especially useful for professionals such as doctors and lawyers.) Finally, there is the *corporation*, which is characterized by transferable ownerships shares, perpetual succession, and, of course, limited liability.

Most small businesses are sole proprietorships, partnerships, or privately-owned corporations. In the past, not many incorporated, since it was necessary to have multiple owners to start a corporation. However, this is changing, since it is now possible in many states for an individual to form a corporation. Note also that the form your business takes is usually not set in stone: A sole proprietorship or partnership can switch to become an LLC as it grows and the risks increase; furthermore, a successful LLC can raise capital by changing its structure to become a corporation and selling stock.

Legal Issues

Many other legal issues besides incorporating (or not) need to be addressed before you start your business. It is impossible to speak directly to every possible business need in this brief appendix, since regulations, licenses, and health and safety codes vary by industry and locality. A restaurant in Manhattan, for instance, has to deal not only with the usual issues such as health inspectors, the state liquor board, but obscure regulations such as New York City's cabaret laws, which prohibit dancing without a license in a place where alcohol is sold. An asbestos-abatement company, on the other hand, has a very different set of standards it has to abide by, including federal regulations. Researching applicable laws is part of starting up any business.

Part of being a wise business owner is knowing when you need help. There is software available for things like bookkeeping, business plans, and Web site creation, but generally, consulting with a knowledgeable professional—an accountant or a lawyer (or both)—is the smartest move. One of the most common mistakes is believing that just because you have expertise in the technical aspects of a certain field, you know all about running a business in that field. Whereas some people may balk at the expense, by suggesting the best way to deal with possible problems, as well as cutting through red tape and seeing possible pitfalls that you may not even have been aware of, such professionals usually more than make up for their cost. After all, they have far more experience at this than does a first-time business owner!

Financial

Another necessary first step in starting a business is obtaining a bank account. However, having the account is not as important as what you do with it. One of the most common problems with small businesses is undercapitalization—especially in brick-and-mortar businesses that sell or make something, rather than service-based businesses. The rule of thumb is that you should have access to money equal to your first year's anticipated profits, plus start-up expenses. (Note that this is not the same as having the money on hand—see the discussion on lines of credit, below.) For instance, if your annual rent, salaries, and equipment will cost $50,000 and you expect $25,000 worth of profit in your first year, you should have access to $75,000 worth of financing.

You need to decide what sort of financing you will need. Small business loans have both advantages and disadvantages. They can provide critical start-up credit, but in order to obtain one, your personal credit will need to be good, and you will, of course, have to pay them off with interest. In general, the more you and your partners put into the business yourselves, the more credit lenders will be willing to extend to you.

Equity can come from your own personal investment, either in cash or an equity loan on your home. You may also want to consider bringing on partners—at least limited financial partners—as a way to cover start-up costs.

It is also worth considering obtaining a line of credit instead of a loan. A loan is taken out all at once, but with a line of credit, you draw on the money as you need it. This both saves you interest payments and means that you have the money you need when you need it. Taking out too large of a loan can be worse than having no money at all! It just sits there collecting interest—or, worse, is spent on something utterly unnecessary—and then is not around when you need it most.

The first five years are the hardest for any business venture; your venture has about double the usual chance of closing in this time (1 out of 6, rather than 1 out of 12). You will probably have to tighten your belt at home, as well as work long hours and keep careful track of your business expenses. Be careful with your money. Do not take unnecessary risks, play it conservatively, and always keep some capital in reserve for emergencies. The hardest part of a new business, of course, is the learning curve of figuring out what, exactly, you need to do to make a profit, and so the best advice is to have plenty of savings—or a job to provide income—while you learn the ropes.

One thing you should not do is count on venture capitalists or "angel investors," that is, businesspeople who make a living investing on other businesses in the hopes that their equity in the company will increase in value. Venture capitalists have gotten something of a reputation as indiscriminate spendthrifts due to some poor choices made during the dot-com boom of the late 1990s, but the fact is that most do not take risks on unproven products. Rather, they are attracted to young companies that have the potential to become regional or national powerhouses and give better-than-average returns. Nor are venture capitalists are endless sources of money; rather, they are savvy businesspeople who are usually attracted to companies that have already experienced a measure of success. Therefore, it is better to rely on your own resources until you have proven your business will work.

Bookkeeping 101

The principles of double-entry bookkeeping have not changed much since its invention in the fifteenth century: one column records debits, and one records credits. The trick is *doing* it. As a small business owner, you need to be disciplined and meticulous at recording your finances. Thankfully, today there is software available that can do everything from tracking payables and receivables to running checks and generating reports.

Honestly ask yourself if you are the sort of person who does a good job keeping track of finances. If you are not, outsource to a bookkeeping company or hire someone to come in once or twice a week to enter invoices and generate checks for you. Also remember that if you have employees or even freelancers, you will have to file tax forms for them at the end of the year.

Another good idea is to have an accountant for your business to handle advice and taxes (federal, state, local, sales tax, etc.). In fact, consulting with an a certified public accountant is a good idea in general, since they are usually aware of laws and rules that you have never even heard of.

Finally, keep your personal and business accounting separate. If your business ever gets audited, the first thing the IRS looks for is personal expenses disguised as business expenses. A good accountant can help you to know what are legitimate business expenses. Everything you take from the business account, such as payroll and reimbursement, must be recorded and classified.

Being an Employer

Know your situation regarding employees. To begin with, if you have any employees, you will need an Employer Identification Number (EIN), also sometimes called a Federal Tax Identification Number. Getting an EIN is simple: You can fill out IRS form SS-4, or complete the process online at http://www.irs.gov.

Having employees carries other responsibilities and legalities with it. To begin with, you will need to pay payroll taxes (otherwise known as "withholding") to cover income tax, unemployment insurance, Social Security, and Medicare, as well as file W-2 and W-4 forms with the government. You will also be required to pay workman's compensation insurance, and will probably also want to find medical insurance. You are also required to abide by your state's nondiscrimination laws. Most states require you to post nondiscrimination and compensation notices in a public area.

Many employers are tempted to unofficially hire workers "off the books." This can have advantages, but can also mean entering a legal gray area. (Note, however, this is different from hiring freelancers, a temp employed by another company, or having a self-employed professional such as an accountant or bookkeeper come in occasionally to provide a service.) It is one thing to hire the neighbor's teenage son on a one-time basis to help you move some boxes, but quite another to have full-time workers working on a cash-and-carry basis. Regular wages must be noted in the accounts, and gaps may be questioned in the event of an audit. If the workers are injured on the job, you are not covered by workman's comp, and are thus vulnerable to lawsuits. If the workers you hired are not legal residents, you can also be liable for civil and criminal penalties. In general, it is best to keep your employees as above-board as possible.

Building a Business

Good business practices are essential to success. First off, do not overextend yourself. Be honest about what you can do and in what time frame. Secondly, be a responsible business owner. In general, if there is a problem, it is best to explain matters honestly to your clients than to leave them without word and wondering. In the former case, there is at least the possibility of salvaging your reputation and credibility.

Most business is still built by personal contacts and word of mouth. It is for this reason that maintaining your list of contacts is an essential practice. Even if a particular contact may not be useful at a particular moment, a future opportunity may present itself—or you may be able to send someone else to them. Networking, in other words, is as important when you are the boss as when you are looking for a job yourself. As the owner of a company, having a network means getting services on better terms, knowing where to go if you need help with a particular problem, or simply being in the right place at the right time to exploit an opportunity. Join professional organizations, the local Chamber of Commerce, clubs and community organizations, and learn to play golf. And remember—never burn a bridge.

Advertising is another way to build a business. Planning an ad campaign is not as difficult as you might think: You probably already know your media market and business community. The trick is applying it. Again, go with your instincts. If you never look twice at your local weekly, other people probably do not, either. If you are in a high-tourist area, though, local tourists maps might be a good way to leverage your marketing dollar. Ask other people in your area or market who have business similar to your own. Depending on your focus, you might want to consider everything from AM radio or local TV networks, to national trade publications, to hiring a PR firm for an all-out blitz. By thinking about these questions, you can spend your advertising dollars most effectively.

Nor should you underestimate the power of using the Internet to build your business. It is a very powerful tool for small businesses, potentially reaching vast numbers of people for relatively little outlay of money. Launching a Web site has become the modern equivalent of hanging out your shingle. Even if you are primarily a brick-and-mortar business, a Web presence can still be an invaluable tool—your store or offices will show up on Google searches, plus customers can find directions to visit you in person. Furthermore, the Internet offers the small-business owner many useful tools. Print and design services, order fulfillment, credit card processing, and networking—both personal and in terms of linking to other sites—are all available online. Web advertising can be useful, too, either by advertising on specialty sites that appeal to your audience, or by using services such as Google AdWords.

Amateurish print ads, TV commercials, and Web sites do not speak well of your business. Good media should be well-designed, well-edited, and well-put together. It need not, however, be expensive. Shop around and, again, use your network.

Flexibility is also important. "In general, a business must adapt to changing conditions, find new customers and find new products or services that customers need when the demand for their older products or services diminishes," says James Peck, a Long Island, New York, entrepreneur. In other words, if your original plan is not working out, or if demand falls, see if you can parlay your experience, skills, and physical plant into meeting other needs. People are not the only ones who can change their path in life; organizations can, too.

A Final Word

In business, as in other areas of life, the advice of more experienced people is essential. "I think it really takes three businesses until you know what you're doing," Drew Curtis confides. "I sure didn't know what I was doing the first time." Listen to what others have to say, no matter whether it is about your Web site or your business plan. One possible solution is seeking out a mentor, someone who has previously launched a successful venture in this field. In any case, before taking any step, ask as many people as many questions as you can. Good advice is invaluable.

Further Resources

American Independent Business Alliance
http://www.amiba.net

American Small Business League
http://www.asbl.com

IRS Small Business and Self-Employed One-Stop Resource
http://www.irs.gov/businesses/small/index.html

The Riley Guide: Steps in Starting Your Own Business
http://www.rileyguide.com/steps.html

Small Business Administration
http://www.sba.gov

Appendix B

Outfitting Yourself for Career Success

As you contemplate a career shift, the first component is to assess your interests. You need to figure out what makes you tick, since there is a far greater chance that you will enjoy and succeed in a career that taps into your passions, inclinations, natural abilities, and training. If you have a general idea of what your interests are, you at least know in which direction you want to travel. You may know you want to simply switch from one sort of nursing to another, or change your life entirely and pursue a dream you have always held. In this case, you can use a specific volume of The Field Guides to Finding a New Career to discover which position to target. If you are unsure of your direction you want to take, well, then the entire scope of the series is open to you! Browse through to see what appeals to you, and see if it matches with your experience and abilities.

The next step you should take is to make a list—do it once in writing—of the skills you have used in a position of responsibility that transfer to the field you are entering. People in charge of interviewing and hiring may well understand that the skills they are looking for in a new hire are used in other fields, but you must spell it out. Most job descriptions are partly a list of skills. Map your experience into that, and very early in your contacts with a prospective employer explicitly address how you acquired your relevant skills. Pick a relatively unimportant aspect of the job to be your ready answer for where you would look forward to learning within the organization, if this seems essentially correct. When you transfer into a field, softly acknowledge a weakness while relating your readiness to learn, but never lose sight of the value you offer both in your abilities and in the freshness of your perspective.

Energy and Experience

The second component in career-switching success is energy. When Jim Fulmer was 61, he found himself forced to close his piano-repair business. However, he was able to parlay his knowledge of music, pianos, and the musical instruments industry into another job as a sales representative for a large piano manufacturer, and quickly built up a clientele of musical-instrument retailers throughout the East Coast. Fulmer's experience highlights another essential lesson for career-changers: There are plenty of opportunities out there, but jobs will not come to you—especially the career-oriented, well-paying ones. You have to seek them out.

Jim Fulmer's case also illustrates another important point: Former training and experience can be a key to success. "Anyone who has to make a career change in any stage of life has to look at what skills they have acquired but may not be aware of," he says. After all, people can more easily change into careers similar to the ones they are leaving. Training and experience also let you enter with a greater level of seniority, provided you have the other necessary qualifications. For instance, a nurse who is already experienced with administering drugs and their benefits and drawbacks, and who is also graced with the personality and charisma to work with the public, can become a pharmaceutical company sales representative.

Unlock Your Network

The next step toward unlocking the perfect job is networking. The term may be overused, but the idea is as old as civilization. More than other animals, humans need one another. With the Internet and telephone, never in history has it been easier to form (or revive) these essential links. One does not have to gird oneself and attend reunion-type events (though for many this is a fine tactic)—but keep open to opportunities to meet people who may be friendly to you in your field. Ben Franklin understood the principal well—*Poor Richard's Almanac* is something of a treatise on the importance or cultivating what Franklin called "friendships" with benefactors. So follow in the steps of the founding fathers and make friends to get ahead. Remember: helping others feels good; it's often the receiving that gets a little tricky. If you know someone particularly well-connected in your field, consider tapping one or two less important connections first so that you make the most of the important one. As you proceed, keep your strengths foremost in your mind because the glue of commerce is mutual interest.

Eighty percent of job openings are *never advertised*, and, according to the U.S. Bureau of Labor statistics, more than half all employees landed their jobs through networking. Using your personal contacts is far more efficient and effective than trusting your résumé to the Web. On the Web, an employer needs to sort through tens of thousands—or millions—of résumés. When you direct your application to one potential employer, you are directing your inquiry to one person who already knows you. The personal touch is everything: Human beings are social animals, programmed to "read" body language; we are naturally inclined to trust those we meet in person, or who our friends and coworkers have recommended. While Web sites can be useful (for looking through help-wanted ads, for instance), expecting employers to pick you out of the slush pile is as effective as throwing your résumé into a black hole.

Do not send your résumé out just to make yourself feel like you're doing something. The proper way to go about things is to employ discipline and order, and then to apply your charm. Begin your networking efforts by making a list of people you can talk to: colleagues, coworkers, and supervisors, people you have had working relationship with, people from church, athletic teams, political organizations, or other community groups, friends, and relatives. You can expand your networking opportunities by following the suggestions in each chapter of the volumes. Your goal here is not so much to land a job as to expand your possibilities and knowledge: Though the people on your list may not be in the position to help you themselves, they might know someone who is. Meeting with them might also help you understand traits that matter and skills that are valued in the field in which you are interested. Even if the person is a potential employer, it is best to phrase your request as if you were seeking information: "You might not be able to help me, but do you know someone I could talk to who could tell me more about what it is like to work in this field?" Being hungry gives one impression, being desperate quite another.

Keep in mind that networking is a two-way street. If you meet someone who had an opening that is not right for you, but if you could recommend someone else, you have just added to your list two people who will be favorably disposed toward you in the future. Also, bear in mind that *you* can help people in *your* old field, thus adding to your own contacts list.

Networking is especially important to the self-employed or those who start their own businesses. Many people in this situation begin because they either recognize a potential market in a field that they are familiar with, or because full-time employment in this industry is no longer a possibility. Already being well-established in a field can help, but so can asking connections for potential work and generally making it known that you are ready, willing, and able to work. Working your professional connections, in many cases, is the *only* way to establish yourself. A freelancer's network, in many cases, is like a spider's web. The spider casts out many strands, since he or she never knows which one might land the next meal.

Dial-Up Help

In general, it is better to call contacts directly than to e-mail them. E-mails are easy for busy people to ignore or overlook, even if they do not mean to. Explain your situation as briefly as possible (see the discussion of the "elevator speech"), and ask if you could meet briefly, either at their office or at a neutral place such as a café. (Be sure that you pay the bill in such a situation—it is a way of showing you appreciate their time and effort.) If you get someone's voicemail, give your "elevator speech" and then say you will call back in a few days to follow up—and then do so. If you reach your contact directly and they are too busy to speak or meet with you, make a definite appointment to call back at a later date. Be persistent, but not annoying.

Once you have arranged a meeting, prep yourself. Look at industry publications both in print and online, as well as news reports (here, GoogleNews, which lets you search through online news reports, can be very handy). Having up-to-date information on industry trends shows that you are dedicated, knowledgeable, and focused. Having specific questions on employers and requests for suggestions will set you apart from the rest of the job-hunting pack. Knowing the score—for instance, asking about the value of one sort of certification instead of another— pegs you as an "insider," rather than a dilettante, someone whose name is worth remembering and passing along to a potential employer.

Finally, set the right mood. Here, a little self-hypnosis goes a long way: Look at yourself in the mirror, and tell yourself that you are an enthusiastic, committed professional. Mood affects confidence and performance. Discipline your mind so you keep your perspective and self-respect. Nobody wants to hire someone who comes across as insincere, tells a sob story, or is still in the doldrums of having lost their previous job. At the end of any networking meeting, ask for someone else who might be able to help you in your journey to finding a position in this field, either with information or a potential job opening.

Get a Lift

When you meet with a contact in person (as well as when you run into anyone by chance who may be able to help you), you need an "elevator speech" (so-named because it should be short enough to be delivered during an elevator ride from a ground level to a high floor). This is a summary in which, in less than two minutes, you give them a clear impression of who you are, where you come from, your experience and goals, and why you are on the path you are on. The motto above Plato's Academy holds true: Know Thyself (this is where our Career Compasses and guides will help you). A long and rambling "elevator story" will get you nowhere. Furthermore, be positive: Neither a sad-sack story nor a tirade explaining how everything that went wrong in your old job is someone else's fault will get you anywhere. However, an honest explanation of a less-than-fortunate circumstance, such as a decline in business forcing an office closing, needing to change residence to a place where you are not qualified to work in order to further your spouse's career, or needing to work fewer hours in order to care for an ailing family member, is only honest.

An elevator speech should show 1) you know the business involved; 2) you know the company; 3) you are qualified (here, try to relate your education and work experience to the new situation); and 4) you are goal-oriented, dependable, and hardworking. Striking a balance is important; you want to sound eager, but not overeager. You also want to show a steady work experience, but not that you have been so narrowly focused that you cannot adjust. Most important is emphasizing what you can do for the company. You will be surprised how much information you can include in two minutes. Practice this speech in front of a mirror until you have the key points down perfectly. It should sound natural, and you should come across as friendly, confident, and assertive. Finally, remember eye contact! Good eye contact needs to be part of your presentation, as well as your everyday approach when meeting potential employers and leads.

Get Your Résumé Ready

Everyone knows what a résumé is, but how many of us have really thought about how to put one together? Perhaps no single part of the job search is subject to more anxiety—or myths and misunderstandings—than this 8 ½-by-11-inch sheet of paper.

On the one hand, it is perfectly all right for someone—especially in certain careers, such as academia—to have a résumé that is more than one page. On the other hand, you do not need to tell a future employer *everything*. Trim things down to the most relevant; for a 40-year-old to mention an internship from two decades ago is superfluous. Likewise, do not include irrelevant jobs, lest you seem like a professional career-changer.

Tailor your descriptions of your former employment to the particular position you are seeking. This is not to say you should lie, but do make your experience more appealing. If the job you're looking for involves supervising other people, say if you have done this in the past; if it involves specific knowledge or capabilities, mention that you possess these qualities. In general, try to make your past experience seem as similar to what you are seeking.

The standard advice is to put your Job Objective at the heading of the résumé. An alternative to this is a Professional Summary, which some recruiters and employers prefer. The difference is that a Job Objective mentions the position you are seeking, whereas a Professional Summary mentions your background (e.g. "Objective: To find a position as a sales representative in agribusiness machinery" versus "Experienced sales representative; strengths include background in agribusiness, as well as building team dynamics and market expansion"). Of course, it is easy to come up with two or three versions of the same document for different audiences.

The body of the résumé of an experienced worker varies a lot more than it does at the beginning of your career. You need not put your education or your job experience first; rather, your résumé should emphasize your strengths. If you have a master's degree in a related field, that might want to go before your unrelated job experience. Conversely, if too much education will harm you, you might want to bury that under the section on professional presentations you have given that show how good you are at communicating. If you are currently enrolled in a course or other professional development, be sure to note this (as well as your date of expected graduation). A résumé is a study of blurs, highlights, and jewels. You blur everything you must in order to fit the description of your experience to the job posting. You highlight what is relevant from each and any of your positions worth mentioning. The jewels are the little headers and such—craft them, since they are what is seen first.

You may also want to include professional organizations, work-related achievements, and special abilities, such as your fluency in a foreign language. Also mention your computer software qualifications and capabilities, especially if you are looking for work in a technological field or if you are an older job-seeker who might be perceived as behind the technology curve. Including your interests or family information might or might not be a good idea—no one really cares about your bridge club, and in fact they might worry that your marathon training might take away from your work commitments, but, on the other hand, mentioning your golf handicap or three children might be a good idea if your potential employer is an avid golfer or is a family woman herself.

You can either include your references or simply note, "References available upon request." However, be sure to ask your references' permission to use their names and alert them to the fact that they may be contacted before you include them on your résumé! Be sure to include name, organization, phone number, and e-mail address for each contact.

Today, word processors make it easy to format your résumé. However, beware of prepackaged résumé "wizards"—they do not make you stand out in the crowd. Feel free to strike out on your own, but remember the most important thing in formatting a résumé is consistency. Unless you have a background in typography, do not get too fancy. Finally, be sure to have someone (or several people!) read your résumé over for you.

For more information on résumé writing, check out Web sites such as http://www.resume.monster.com.

Craft Your Cover Letter

It is appropriate to include a cover letter with your résumé. A cover letter lets you convey extra information about yourself that does not fit or is not always appropriate in your résumé, such as why you are no longer working in your original field of employment. You can and should also mention the name of anyone who referred you to the job. You can go into some detail about the reason you are a great match, given the job description. Also address any questions that might be raised in the potential employer's mind (for instance, a gap in employment). Do not, however, ramble on. Your cover letter should stay focused on your goal: To offer a strong, positive impression of yourself and persuade the hiring manager that you are worth an interview. Your cover letter gives you a chance to stand out from the other applicants and sell yourself. In fact, according to a CareerBuilder.com survey, 23 percent of hiring managers say a candidate's ability to relate his or her experience to the job at hand is a top hiring consideration.

Even if you are not a great writer, you can still craft a positive yet concise cover letter in three paragraphs: An introduction containing the specifics of the job you are applying for; a summary of why you are a good fit for the position and what you can do for the company; and a closing with a request for an interview, contact information, and thanks. Remember to vary the structure and tone of your cover letter—do not begin every sentence with "I."

Ace Your Interview

In truth, your interview begins well before you arrive. Be sure to have read up well on the company and its industry. Use Web sites and magazines—http://www.hoovers.com offers free basic business information, and trade magazines deliver both information and a feel for the industries they cover. Also, do not neglect talking to people in your circle who might know about trends in the field. Leave enough time to digest the information so that you can give some independent thought to the company's history and prospects. You don't need to expert when you arrive to be interviewed; but you should be comfortable. The most important element of all is to be poised and relaxed during the interview itself. Preparation and practice can help a lot.

Be sure to develop well-thought-through answers to the following, typical interview openers and standard questsions.

☞ Tell me about yourself. (Do not complain about how unsatisfied you were in your former career, but give a brief summary of your applicable background and interest in the particular job area.) If there is a basis to it, emphasize how much you love to work and how you are a team player.

☞ Why do you want this job? (Speak from the brain, and the heart—of course you want the money, but say a little here about what you find interesting about the field and the company's role in it.)

☞ What makes you a good hire? (Remember here to connect the company's needs and your skill set. Ultimately, your selling points probably come down to one thing: you will make your employer money. You want the prospective hirer to see that your skills are valuable not to the world in general but to this specific company's bottom line. What can you do for them?)

☞ What led you to leave your last job? (If you were fired, still try say something positive, such as, "The business went through a challenging time, and some of the junior marketing people were let go.")

Practice answering these and other questions, and try to be genuinely positive about yourself, and patient with the process. Be secure but not cocky; don't be shy about forcing the focus now and then on positive contributions you have made in your working life—just be specific. As with the elevator speech, practice in front of the mirror.

A couple pleasantries are as natural a way as any to start the actual interview, but observe the interviewer closely for any cues to fall silent and formally begin. Answer directly; when in doubt, finish your phrase and look to the interviewer. Without taking command, you can always ask, "Is there more you would like to know?" Your attentiveness will convey respect. Let your personality show too—a positive attitude and a grounded sense of your abilities will go a long way to getting you considered. During the interview, keep your cell phone off and do not look at your watch. Toward the end of your meeting, you may be asked whether you have any questions. It is a good idea to have one or two in mind. A few examples follow:

☞ "What makes your company special in the field?"

☞ "What do you consider the hardest part of this position?"

☞ "Where are your greatest opportunities for growth?"

☞ "Do you know when you might need anything further from me?"

Leave discussion of terms for future conversations. Make a cordial, smooth exit.

Remember to Follow Up

Send a thank-you note. Employers surveyed by CareerBuilder.com in 2005 said it matters. About 15 percent said they would not hire someone who did not follow up with a thanks. And almost 33 percent would think less of a candidate. The form of the note does not much matter—if you know a manager's preference, use it. Otherwise, just be sure to follow up.

Winning an Offer

A job offer can feel like the culmination of a long and difficult struggle. So naturally, when you hear them, you may be tempted to jump at the offer. Don't. Once an employer wants you, he or she will usually give you a chance to consider the offer. This is the time to discuss terms of employment, such as vacation, overtime, and benefits. A little effort now can be well worth it in the future. Be sure to do a check of prevailing salaries for your field and area before signing on. Web sites for this include Payscale.com, Salary.com, and Salaryexpert.com. If you are thinking about asking for better or different terms from what the prospective employer offered, rest assured—that's how business gets done; and it may just burnish the positive impression you have already made.

Index